INTERNATIONAL DEVELOPMENT IN FOCUS

The Global Health Cost of PM$_{2.5}$ Air Pollution

A Case for Action Beyond 2021

Contents

Figures

Tables

Acknowledgments

This report was prepared by a team led by Yewande Awe with the core team comprising Bjorn Larsen and Ernesto Sánchez-Triana. The task team also included Santiago Enriquez and Shafick Hoossein. This report updates the "2020 Cost of Air Pollution" report by using health data for the Global Burden of Disease study published at the end of 2020.

The team would like to acknowledge, with thanks, the valuable advice and inputs of the following colleagues: Stephen Dorey, Fernando Loayza, Helena Naber, Katelijn Van den Berg, and Martin Heger (World Bank); and Maureen Cropper (Professor of Economics, University of Maryland). Editorial support was provided by Stan Wanat.

This report is a product of the Environment, Natural Resources, and Blue Economy Global Practice of the World Bank. This work was conducted under the supervision of Juergen Voegele (Vice President, Sustainable Development Practice Group); Karin Kemper (Global Director, Environment, Natural Resources, and Blue Economy); Richard Damania (Chief Economist, Sustainable Development Practice Group); Iain Shuker (Practice Manager, Africa, Environment, Natural Resources, and Blue Economy); and Christian Albert Peter (Practice Manager, Global Engagement, Environment, Natural Resources, and Blue Economy).

The Pollution Management and Environmental Health Multi-donor Trust Fund of the World Bank provided financial support for the preparation of this report. That support is gratefully acknowledged.

Preface

In 2020, as cities around the world went into COVID-19-induced lockdowns, people took notice of the surprisingly blue skies above them. By painfully grinding economic and social activities to a halt, lockdowns resulted in rapid reductions of air pollutants. However, in most cities, air pollution returned to its pre-pandemic levels almost as soon as restrictions were eased. This was a stark reminder of the need to strengthen efforts to tackle air pollution and to integrate air-pollution reductions into countries' recovery efforts.

According to the Global Burden of Disease 2019, $PM_{2.5}$ (fine particulate matter) air pollution—in both outdoor environments and inside households that use solid fuels for cooking and heating—caused 6.4 million deaths and 93 billion days lived with illness in 2019. While the toll of various risks, including household air pollution, has fallen over time, that of ambient air pollution has continued to rise over the last decade.

The significant health, social, and economic effects of air pollution compel us to support client countries in addressing air pollution as a core development challenge. To this end, the Bank is committed to continue strengthening the evidence base that can inform effective and efficient air-quality interventions. Recent groundbreaking research advanced by the Bank has made substantial contributions to this evidence base in areas that include (a) the importance of prioritizing efforts to reduce air-pollution emissions from coal-fired power plants and diesel-fueled vehicles because the particles in those emissions are more damaging to health than particles from most other air-pollution sources (Thurston, Awe, Ostro and Sánchez-Triana 2021); (b) demonstrating that particulate matter from dust should continue to be factored into global estimates of the burden of disease of air pollution given the substantial health impact of dust (Ostro, Awe, and Sánchez-Triana 2021); and (c) building a strong case for scaling up efforts to establish ground-level networks for monitoring air quality in low- and middle-income countries by demonstrating that satellite-based air-quality estimates are not a sufficiently accurate substitute for ground-level data (World Bank 2021).

This publication aims to further contribute to the evidence base on air-quality management by providing up-to-date estimates of the global economic costs of air pollution. The analysis builds on previous estimates by the Bank and its partners and is based on cutting-edge scientific findings of the health effects of air pollution, as well as more comprehensive air-quality data from monitoring stations in a large number of cities across the world.

By providing monetary estimates of the health damage of air pollution, this publication aims to support policy makers and decision-makers in client countries to prioritize air pollution amid competing development challenges. Its findings build a strong economic case to invest scarce budgetary resources in the design and implementation of policies and interventions to improve air quality that will deliver benefits for societies at large, and particularly for vulnerable groups.

REFERENCES

GBD 2019 Risk Factors Collaborators. 2020. "Global Burden of 87 Risk Factors in 204 Countries and Territories, 1990 -2019: A Systematic Analysis for the Global Burden of Disease Study 2019." *Lancet* 396: 1223 -49.

Ostro, Bart, Yewande Awe, and Ernesto Sánchez-Triana. 2021. *When the Dust Settles: A Review of the Health Implications of the Dust Component of Air Pollution.* Washington, DC: World Bank.

Thurston, George, Yewande Awe, Bart Ostro, and Ernesto Sanchez-Triana. 2021. "Are All Air Pollution Particles Equal? How Constituents and Sources of Fine Air Pollution Particles (PM2.5) Affect Health." A World Bank Study. World Bank, Washington, DC.

World Bank. 2021. *Getting Down to Earth: Are Satellites Reliable for Measuring Air Pollutants that Cause Mortality in Low- and Middle-Income Countries?* International Development in Focus. Washington, DC: World Bank.

About This Work

The analytical work in this report builds on a growing body of evidence that the World Bank is building to better understand the linkages between air pollution and health, strengthen quantification of the health damage from air pollution, and support improved air quality monitoring and data in low- and middle-income countries. Recent contributions from this body of work include (1) the monetary valuation of the global cost of mortality and morbidity caused by exposure to ambient $PM_{2.5}$ air pollution, (2) demonstration that the dust component of air pollution has substantial health effects and should thus continue to be factored into global estimates of the health burden of air pollution, and (3) demonstration of the importance of prioritizing efforts to reduce air pollution emissions from coal-fired power plants and diesel-fueled vehicles because their particles are more damaging to health than particles from most other air pollution sources.

Executive Summary

INTRODUCTION

Air pollution is a major cause of disease and death. "Ambient air pollution" refers to air pollution in the outdoor air; "household air pollution" refers to air pollution originating in the household environment. Air pollution is the world's leading environmental risk to health and the cause of morbidity and mortality from diseases such as ischemic heart disease, stroke, lung cancer, chronic obstructive pulmonary disease, pneumonia, type 2 diabetes, and neonatal disorders. Most deaths related to air pollution are caused by human exposure to fine inhalable particles or fine particulate matter, also known as $PM_{2.5}$.

Billions of people in developing countries live in places where the ambient and indoor concentrations of $PM_{2.5}$ are multiple times higher than the health-based guideline values for air quality established by the World Health Organization (WHO). An estimated 6.4 million people died prematurely worldwide in 2019 due to exposure to $PM_{2.5}$ air pollution. About 95 percent of those deaths occurred in low- and middle-income countries (LMICs) (GBD 2019 study[1]). Seventy percent of the deaths occurred in East Asia and the Pacific, and South Asia. China and India accounted for 52 percent of global deaths from $PM_{2.5}$. There were six countries with more than 100,000 deaths from $PM_{2.5}$, and nine countries with 50,000–100,000 deaths.

Besides being a health problem, air pollution contributes to less-livable conditions and hinders economic competitiveness. Poor people are more likely to live in a polluted environment and suffer the adverse impacts of air pollution. In addition, people who are sick as a result of exposure to air pollution are more likely to take days off work and suffer reduced productivity, which in turn undermines their contributions to economic growth. Air pollution could also hinder cities' ability to attract talented workers, thereby reducing competitiveness. Furthermore, air pollution imposes a heavy economic burden both on the economies of individual LMICs and on the global economy as a result of illness, premature death, lost earnings, and increased health-care expenditures—all of which constrain productivity and economic growth. Poor people who have the least means to address the health damage of air pollution often disproportionately carry the economic burden.

Air pollution is also associated with many detrimental, but less researched, health impacts and conditions (Sánchez-Triana et al. 2015), such as infant mortality (Heft-Neal et al. 2018), low birth weight (Ezziane 2013), pre-term delivery (Bowe et al. 2018), mental health conditions (Shin Park, and Choi 2018), and neurological impairment (Xu, Ha, and Basnet 2016; Zhang, Chen, and Zhang 2018) including dementia in later life (Carey et al. 2018). As the evidence base for these and other conditions becomes stronger, it is envisaged that exposure-response functions can be developed to obtain global estimates of the health burden of air pollution.

Some air pollutants, notably short-lived climate pollutants, such as black carbon, have climate-warming properties (Shindell et al. 2012). In addition, air pollution (particularly linked to sulfur dioxide) adversely affects the environment, resulting in acid rain and associated land and water pollution. Air pollution also has aesthetic impacts, such as reduced visibility. However, economic valuation of these impacts can be done only at local and regional levels. Further research is needed to determine how to effectively conduct economic valuation of these impacts at the global level.

Air pollution's various adverse impacts on multiple facets of the society and economy, particularly of LMICs, squarely place air pollution as a core development challenge. This makes reducing air pollution in developing countries central to achieving poverty reduction and equitable prosperity objectives in those countries.

Global health crises further highlight the need for continued action in addressing a global and cross-cutting challenge such as air pollution. The current global COVID-19 pandemic, caused by the novel coronavirus, SARS-CoV-2, underscores the importance of reducing air pollution through preventive and abatement measures. People who contract COVID-19 and have underlying medical problems such as heart disease, lung disease, and cancer are at a higher risk of developing serious illnesses that could lead to death. It is noteworthy that air pollution is a cause of the aforementioned diseases. Ongoing research is finding relationships between air pollution and the incidence of illness and death due to COVID-19. Such research suggests that PM$_{2.5}$ air pollution plays an important role in increased COVID-19 incidence and death rates. One such study reported that PM$_{2.5}$ is a highly significant predictor of the number of confirmed cases of COVID-19 and related hospital admissions (Andrée 2020).

MOTIVATION

This report provides an estimate of the global, regional, and national costs of health damage—that is, premature mortality and morbidity—from exposure to PM$_{2.5}$ air pollution in 2019. While recognizing the various costs of air pollution to society, this report focuses on the cost of premature mortality and morbidity of health effects estimated by the GBD 2019 study. Estimating the health damage of air pollution in monetary terms provides a suitable metric for policy makers and decision makers in developing countries to prioritize the design and implementation of policies and interventions for controlling air pollution amid competing development challenges and budgetary and other resource constraints. An earlier study by the World Bank and IHME (2016) estimated the cost of premature mortality from ambient air pollution and household air pollution combined in 2013.[2]

The present report estimates the cost of health damages using the estimates of mortality and morbidity from $PM_{2.5}$ air pollution published in the Global Burden of Disease (GBD) 2019 study. The GBD assesses mortality and disability from numerous diseases, injuries, and risk factors, including air pollution. Air pollution has long been recognized as a significant environmental health risk. GBD estimates of the global, regional, and national health burden attributable to air pollution, based on nationwide exposures to ambient $PM_{2.5}$ as well as household use of solid fuels, were published for the first time in the GBD 2010 study, followed by GBD 2013, 2015, 2016, 2017, and 2019.

METHODOLOGY

This report uses the GBD 2019 estimates of premature mortality and morbidity attributable to $PM_{2.5}$ air pollution to value the economic cost in dollar terms. The GBD estimates the major health damages of population exposure to $PM_{2.5}$ from exposure-response relationships that have been established by global research on air pollution and health. These exposure-response relationships provide estimates of the number of cases of premature deaths and disease in a country that result from the population's exposure to given concentrations of $PM_{2.5}$. Population-exposure levels to ambient $PM_{2.5}$ are estimated based on a combination of ground-level monitoring of ambient $PM_{2.5}$, satellite imagery, and chemical-transport models. Population-exposure levels to $PM_{2.5}$ household air pollution are estimated based on population use of solid fuels for cooking and other domestic purposes, combined with household $PM_{2.5}$ measurements, type of solid fuel and cookstove, urban-rural household location, and sociodemographic characteristics known to influence household air-pollution levels.

The cost of the health damages from $PM_{2.5}$ air pollution is quantified separately for premature deaths and morbidity. The cost of premature deaths is estimated from the value of statistical life (VSL). VSL is a measure of how much individuals are willing to pay for a reduction in the risk or likelihood of premature death. VSL is influenced by income level and other factors; it is unique for each country. The cost of morbidity is estimated based on years lived with disability (YLDs) estimated by the GBD. YLD is a measure of disease burden that reflects the duration and severity of diseases. YLDs from exposure to $PM_{2.5}$ are converted to days lived with disease, with the cost of a day of disease equated to a fraction of the average daily wage rate in each country.

This report recognizes that $PM_{2.5}$ comes from both natural (for example, dust) and anthropogenic (for example, vehicle exhausts, emissions from power generation, and household use of solid fuels) origins to varying extents. The epidemiologic literature indicates that short- and long-term exposures to dust have significant health impacts and provides a reasonable basis to assume that the health risk per microgram of natural dust is generally similar to that of other constituents of $PM_{2.5}$, with the exception of sulfates and elemental carbon (Ostro et al. 2021). Epidemiologic evidence supports inclusion of the effects of natural dust on mortality and morbidity in the quantification of health impacts of ambient air pollution. Furthermore, while global studies of health impacts of $PM_{2.5}$ have been based on particle mass, the epidemiologic evidence shows that adverse health damages of $PM_{2.5}$ vary according to $PM_{2.5}$ source and composition. Specifically, trace constituents from $PM_{2.5}$ and $PM_{2.5}$ mass from fossil-fuel combustion are among the greatest contributors to $PM_{2.5}$ toxicity (Thurston et al. 2021). Estimation of health impacts of natural dust, PM$_{2.5}$ constituents and PM$_{2.5}$ mass from different sources, at a global level, will require strengthening the measurement of PM$_{2.5}$ constituents and source-markers, and improved understanding of exposure-response relationships. In this report, the valuation of health damage from PM$_{2.5}$ is based on PM$_{2.5}$ mass and is not disaggregated by PM$_{2.5}$ source or constituent (Ostro et al. 2021).

KEY FINDINGS

- The global health cost of mortality and morbidity caused by exposure to PM$_{2.5}$ air pollution in 2019 was $8.1 trillion, equivalent to 6.1 percent of global gross domestic product (GDP).[3] The cost ranged from an equivalent of 1.7 percent of GDP in North America, to 9.3 percent in East Asia and Pacific, and 10.3 percent in South Asia (figure ES.1). The cost was equivalent to

FIGURE ES.1

Cost of health damage from PM$_{2.5}$ exposure in 2019 by region, percent equivalent of GDP (PPP)

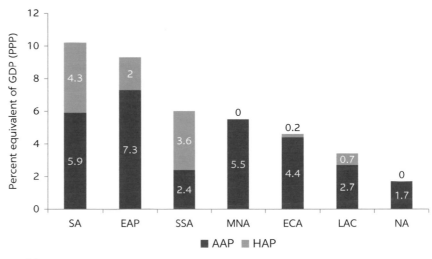

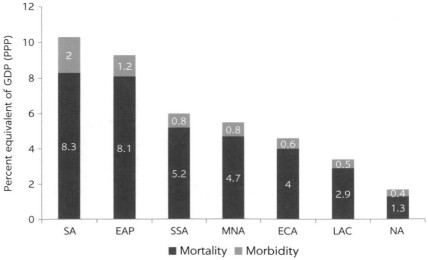

Source: Original calculations for this publication.
Note: EAP = East Asia and Pacific; ECA = Europe and Central Asia; LAC = Latin America and Caribbean; MNA = Middle East and North Africa, NA = North America; SA = South Asia; SSA = Sub-Saharan Africa. Numbers may not add up due to rounding.

5.9 percent of GDP in low-income countries and rose to 8.9–9.0 percent in lower- and upper-middle-income countries (figure ES.2). The cost was equivalent to 10.6–12.9 percent of GDP in China and India.

- Globally, 64 percent of total deaths from $PM_{2.5}$ was due to ambient air pollution and 36 percent due to household air pollution from the use of solid fuels. However, the cost of household air pollution constituted the largest share in Sub-Saharan Africa and low-income countries, a substantial share in South Asia and lower-middle-income countries, and a moderate share in East Asia and Pacific, Latin America and Caribbean, and upper-middle-income countries.

- Of the estimated total global health cost of $PM_{2.5}$ air pollution, about 85 percent is due to premature mortality and 15 percent to morbidity.

- The estimated global cost of $PM_{2.5}$ air pollution in 2019 is 40 percent higher than the estimate for 2013 in World Bank and IHME (2016) in real terms. The higher cost estimate in this report is related to three sets of factors:

FIGURE ES.2

Annual cost of health damage from $PM_{2.5}$ exposure, as a share of GDP by income group, 2019

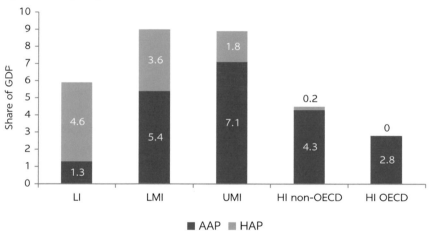

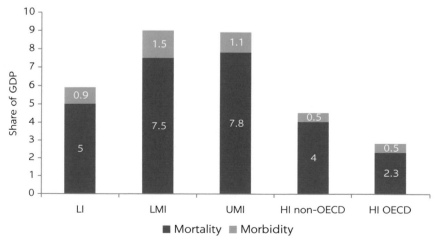

Source: Original calculations for this publication.
Note: LI = low-income countries; LMI = lower-middle-income countries; UMI = upper-middle-income countries; and HI = high-income countries. PM2.5 = fine particulate matter. OECD = Organisaton for Economic Co-operation and Development. Assignment of countries to categories based on World Bank income classification. Numbers may not add up due to rounding.

- Improved methodology: This report uses updated exposure-response functions from the GBD 2019, which quantitatively relate exposure levels of PM$_{2.5}$ to the risk of a health damage (chronic obstructive pulmonary disease, stroke, ischemic heart disease, lower respiratory infection, lung cancer, and type 2 diabetes). The GBD 2019 also includes neonatal health effects of PM$_{2.5}$ exposure. Type 2 diabetes and neonatal health effects were not included in the GBD 2013.
  - Increased availability of data: Ground-level ambient PM measurements utilized by the GBD 2019 study came from the updated World Health Organization (WHO) Global Ambient Air Quality Database released in 2018, as well as additional data mainly from Bangladesh, Canada, China, the European Union, the United States, and PM measurement data from US embassies and consulates. Thus, measurement data from 10,408 ground monitors from 116 countries were utilized by the GBD 2019.
  - Inclusion of an estimate of the cost of morbidity, which was not provided in World Bank and IHME (2016).
- Observations about the reasons for variations between GBD mortality estimates for different years were noted in Ostro et al. (2018), which examined estimates provided in GBD 2010, GBD 2013, and GBD 2015 of mortality related to air pollution. Methodological and technological improvements and demographic changes were found to account for the observed variations in the mortality estimates. Ostro et al. (2018) also noted the need to strengthen ground-level air-quality monitoring and epidemiological studies to improve estimates of PM$_{2.5}$ exposure and mortality in LMICs that are related to air pollution.
- Although the global availability of exposure data in GBD 2019 increased due to increased ground-level monitoring data, there remains a great need to increase ground-level air-quality measurements in LMICs in order to reduce uncertainties regarding PM$_{2.5}$ exposure estimates in countries that have limited or no ground-level measurements, particularly of PM$_{2.5}$. Analysis of the WHO Global Ambient Air Quality Database 2018 version reveals that there was only one PM$_{2.5}$ ground-level monitor per 65 million people in low-income countries, and one monitor per 28 million people in Sub-Saharan Africa, in contrast to one monitor per 370,000 people in high-income countries.

Recommendations for policy action

The significant health and economic burdens of PM$_{2.5}$ air pollution call for urgent action from policy makers in LMICs to reduce air pollution and the resulting disease and deaths. Some key areas for action include the following:

- **Improve ground-level air-quality monitoring.** Properly operated and maintained ground-level monitoring networks for air quality provide data on the severity of air pollution, a fundamental input for effective air-quality management. Data for networks that monitor air quality are also useful for identifying the key sources that contribute to ambient air pollution. Such networks for air-quality monitoring must be subject to rigorous quality-assurance and quality-control regimes in order to ensure that the air-quality measurements generated are reliable for informing the design and implementation of interventions to reduce air pollution and protect public health. Thus, high-quality, routine air-quality monitoring, first and foremost, underpins programs for effective air-quality management that would also include (a) comprehensive emission inventories; (b) application of models to understand the transport and fate of air pollutants; (c) assessment of costs and of health and other benefits; and (d) public outreach and stakeholder engagement. It is pertinent to note that beyond initial investments in networks for air-quality monitoring, governments need to ensure effective funding for sustained operation and maintenance of programs for air-quality monitoring in the long term.

- **Ensure public access to information on air quality.** To reinforce the impact of networks for air-quality monitoring, air-quality management efforts should include a robust system for public dissemination of air-quality data in formats that are widely understood and easily accessible to members of the public. Public dissemination of air-quality data allows members of the public to take adequate measures to reduce their exposure to air pollution and thus provides an important social safety net for the public—particularly for vulnerable groups such as young children, the elderly, and people with health conditions that can be exacerbated by poor air quality.

- **Harness innovation to drive air-quality improvements.** Technological developments can support more-targeted interventions for air-quality management while providing new avenues to engage local communities in their implementation. For instance, the Environmental Defense Fund and partners such as Google are piloting the use of low-cost sensing technologies and data analytics to provide air-quality data with a significantly higher frequency (every minute or few minutes) and resolution (for example, city block by city block). These hyperlocal monitoring networks can identify areas of poor air quality that a sparse network of traditional monitors often misses, help to better estimate actual exposure to air pollution, and even provide real-time data to help vulnerable populations make decisions that will protect their health.

- **Establish solid technical units with a clear mandate for air-quality management.** Technical units, staffed with specialists who can carry out a range of actions, including monitoring, enforcement, and planning, are indispensable to improve air quality. Such units should have clear responsibilities for designing air-quality interventions that can be endorsed by decision-makers and other stakeholders, as well as for conducting regular evaluations to assess the efficiency and effectiveness of supported interventions, identify opportunities for improvement, and incorporate new scientific evidence or emerging technologies that can drive air-quality improvements. Providing technical units with the mandate to work across sectors is paramount, given that air pollution originates from a wide range of sectors, including energy, transportation, industry, and agriculture, among others.

- **Adopt regional approaches to address air pollution across boundaries.** Air pollution typically cuts across boundaries of individual cities or countries. As a result, regional airshed approaches to addressing $PM_{2.5}$ air pollution may be called for, which require federal and international collaboration of governments across multiple administrative jurisdictions and geographical boundaries to ensure effective air-quality management.

- **Prioritize key sources of $PM_{2.5}$ air pollution, notably fossil-fuel combustion, such as sulfur-emitting coal-fired power plants and diesel-fueled traffic.** Efforts to control air pollution that prioritize fossil-fuel combustion sources are most likely to return greater health benefits than broad efforts that do not consider the source and composition of $PM_{2.5}$. Sulfate—a chemical constituent of $PM_{2.5}$ from coal burning—is one of the greatest contributors to

PM$_{2.5}$ toxicity and has one of the strongest associations with cardiovascular disease among the chemical constituents of PM$_{2.5}$ from fossil-fuel combustion. Reductions in PM$_{2.5}$ emissions from fossil-fuel combustion, such as sulfur-emitting coal-fired power plants and diesel vehicles, can be expected to produce the most-significant health benefits per unit of PM$_{2.5}$ reduced. Given that these sources are also key contributors to climate warming, air-pollution efforts that target these sources will also provide benefits to mitigating climate change. Notably, reducing PM$_{2.5}$ also means reducing black carbon, a component of PM$_{2.5}$ and short-lived climate pollutant.

- **Engage a wide range of instruments that are suited to effectively and efficiently reduce air pollution and ensure that their use is enforced.** In order to reduce air pollution, governments need to apply the instruments and approaches that are most effective for reducing air pollution. Command-and-control instruments (such as standards for ambient air quality and emission standards for vehicles and stationary sources, and vehicle inspection and maintenance programs) are well established and applied in many countries. Additional command-and-control instruments include regulations to improve fuel quality by, for example, decreasing the sulfur content of fuels. Economic instruments (such as air-pollution charges and repurposing of fossil-fuel subsidies) reduce air and climate pollutants while also augmenting the amount of government revenues that can be allocated to education, healthcare, renewable energy, and interventions to control air pollution. In addition, policies to promote conversion of vehicles from diesel to gas or to discourage the use of nitrogen-based fertilizers (which release ammonia—a precursor of secondary PM$_{2.5}$ formation) may also be used to reduce air pollution. It is important to note that effective application of the various instruments for air-quality management requires that governments put in place adequate enforcement mechanisms that also include incentives to reduce polluting behaviors.

- **Promote the use of clean cooking fuels to combat the health effects of household air pollution from solid fuels.** The populations in low- and middle-income countries using traditional cookstoves with solid fuels for cooking and other domestic purposes are exposed to PM$_{2.5}$ concentrations that are several times higher than ambient PM$_{2.5}$. Improved cookstoves, often 40–60 percent more energy efficient than traditional stoves, have been found to reduce exposure by around 50 percent. This reduction, however, reduces health effects by as little as 11–12 percent, based on analysis of the exposure-response functions from the GBD 2019. Effectively combating the health effects requires clean cooking fuels and technologies, such as LPG or electricity. Some low- and middle-income countries have already achieved a high prevalence rate of the population using clean fuels and technologies, demonstrating this possibility even at moderate GDP per capita levels.

NOTES

1. The GBD 2019 study is listed in the references sections of this report as GBD 2019 Risk Factors Collaborators (2020).

2. Total air pollution damages in World Bank and IHME (2016) included ambient PM$_{2.5}$, household PM$_{2.5}$, and ambient ozone.

3. Global health cost and GDP are stated in purchasing power parity (PPP) adjusted US$. GDP in PPP-adjusted US$ allows for a comparison of the purchasing power of GDP of different countries. The global health cost is expressed as a percentage of GDP only to provide a convenient sense of relative scale.

REFERENCES

Andrée, P. J. 2020. "Incidence of COVID-19 and Connections with Air Pollution Exposure: Evidence from the Netherlands." Policy Research Working Paper 9221, Washington, DC, World Bank.

Bowe, B., Y. Xie, T. Li, Y. Yan, H. Xian, and Z. Al-Aly. 2018. "The 2016 Global and National Burden of Diabetes Mellitus Attributable to $PM_{2.5}$ Air Pollution." *Lancet Planetary Health* 2 (7): e301–e312.

Carey, I. M., H. R. Anderson, R. W. Atkinson, S. D. Beevers, D. G. Cook, D. P. Strachan, D. Dajnak, J. Gulliver, and F. J. Kelly. 2018. "Are Noise and Air Pollution Related to the Incidence of Dementia? A Cohort Study in London, England." *BMJ Open* 8: e022404.

Ezziane, Z. 2013. "The Impact of Air Pollution on Low Birth Weight and Infant Mortality." *Review of Environmental Health* 28 (2–3): 107–15.

GBD 2013 Risk Factors Collaborators. 2015. "Global, Regional, and National Comparative Risk Assessment of 79 Behavioural, Environmental and Occupational, and Metabolic Risks or Clusters of Risks in 188 Countries, 1990–2013: A Systematic Analysis for the Global Burden of Disease Study 2013." *Lancet* 386: 2287–323.

GBD 2015 Risk Factors Collaborators. 2016. "Global, Regional, and National Comparative Risk Assessment of 79 Behavioural, Environmental and Occupational, and Metabolic Risks or Clusters of Risks, 1990–2015: A Systematic Analysis for the Global Burden of Disease Study 2015." *Lancet* 388: 1659–724.

GBD 2016 Risk Factors Collaborators. 2017. "Global, Regional, and National Comparative Risk Assessment of 84 Behavioural, Environmental and Occupational, and Metabolic Risks or Clusters of Risks, 1990–2016: A Systematic Analysis for the Global Burden of Disease Study 2016." *Lancet* 390: 1345–422.

GBD 2017 Risk Factors Collaborators. 2018. "Global, Regional, and National Comparative Risk Assessment of 84 Behavioural, Environmental and Occupational, and Metabolic Risks or Clusters of Risks for 195 Countries and Territories, 1990–2017: A Systematic Analysis for the Global Burden of Disease Study 2017." *Lancet* 392: 1923–94.

GBD 2019 Risk Factors Collaborators. 2020. "Global Burden of 87 Risk Factors in 204 Countries and Territories, 1990–2019: A Systematic Analysis for the Global Burden of Disease Study 2019." *Lancet* 396: 1223–49.

Heft-Neal, S., J. Burney, E. Bendavid, and M. Burk. 2018. "Robust Relationship Between Air Quality and Infant Mortality in Africa." *Nature* 559 (7713): 254–58.

Ostro, Bart, Yewande Awe, and Ernesto Sánchez-Triana. 2021. *When the Dust Settles: A Review of the Health Implications of the Dust Component of Air Pollution*. Washington, DC: World Bank.

Ostro, B., J. V. Spadaro, S. Gumy, P. Mudu, Y. Awe, F. Forastiere, and A. Peters. 2018. "Assessing the Recent Estimates of the Global Burden of Disease for Ambient Air Pollution: Methodological Changes and Implications for Low- and Middle-Income Countries." *Environmental Research* 166: 713–25.

Sánchez-Triana, E., S. Enriquez, B. Larsen, P. Webster, and J. Afzal. 2015. *Sustainability and Poverty Alleviation: Confronting Environmental Threats in Sindh, Pakistan*. Directions in Development. Washington, DC: World Bank.

Shin J., J. Y. Park, and J. Choi. 2018. "Long-Term Exposure to Ambient Air Pollutants and Mental Health Status. A Nationwide Population-Based Cross-Sectional Study." *PLOS One* 13 (4): e0195607.

Shindell, D., J. C. I. Kuylenstierna, E. Vignati, R. van Dingenen, M. Amann, Z. Klimont, S. C. Anenberg, N. Muller, G. Janssens-Maenhout, F. Raes, J. Schwartz, G. Faluvegi, L. Pozzoli, K. Kupiainen, L. Höglund-Isaksson, L. Emberson, D. Streets, V. Ramanathan, K. Hicks, N. T. K. Oanh, G. Milly, M. Williams, V. Demkine, and D. Fowler. 2012. "Simultaneously Mitigating Near-Term Climate Change and Improving Human Health and Food Security." *Science* 335: 183–89.

Thurston, George, Yewande Awe, Bart Ostro, and Ernesto Sanchez-Triana. 2021. *Are All Air Pollution Particles Equal? How Constituents and Sources of Fine Air Pollution Particles (PM$_{2.5}$) Affect Health*. World Bank, Washington, DC.

World Bank. 2021. *Getting Down to Earth: Are Satellites Reliable for Measuring Air Pollutants that Cause Mortality in Low- and Middle-Income Countries?* International Development in Focus. Washington, DC: World Bank.

World Bank and IHME (Institute for Health Metrics and Evaluation). 2016. *The Cost of Air Pollution: Strengthening the Economic Case for Action*. Washington, DC: World Bank.

Xu, X., S. U. Ha, and R. Basnet 2016. "A Review of Epidemiological Research on Adverse Neurological Effects of Exposure to Ambient Air Pollution." *Frontiers in Public Health* 4: 157.

Zhang, X., X. Chen, and X. Zhang. 2018. "The Impact of Exposure to Air Pollution on Cognitive Performance." *Proceedings of the National Academy of Sciences* 115 (37): 9193–97.

Abbreviations

AAP	ambient air pollution
COI	cost of illness
COPD	chronic obstructive pulmonary disease
EAP	East Asia and Pacific
ECA	Europe and Central Asia
GBD	Global Burden of Disease
GDP	gross domestic product
HAP	household air pollution
HI	high-income
IER	Integrated Exposure-Response
IHD	ischemic heart disease
IHME	Institute for Health Metrics and Evaluation
LAC	Latin America and the Caribbean
LI	low-income
LMI	lower-middle-income
LMICs	low- and middle-income countries
LRI	lower respiratory infection
MNA	Middle East and North Africa
NA	North America
OECD	Organisation for Economic Co-operation and Development
PM	particulate matter
$PM_{2.5}$	fine particles (particles with a diameter of 2.5 micrometers or less)
PM_{10}	inhalable particles (particles with a diameter of 10 micrometers or less)
PPP	purchasing power parity
RR	relative risks
SA	South Asia
SSA	Sub-Saharan Africa
UMI	upper-middle-income
VSL	value of statistical life
WHO	World Health Organization
WTP	willingness to pay
YLDs	years lived with disability

1 Introduction and Objectives

The detrimental effects of air pollution, notably $PM_{2.5}$ air pollution, to health are well known. "Ambient air pollution" refers to air pollution in the outdoor air; "household air pollution" refers to air pollution originating in the household environment. Air pollution is the world's leading environmental risk to health and the cause of morbidity and mortality from diseases such as ischemic heart disease (IHD), stroke, lung cancer, chronic obstructive pulmonary disease (COPD), pneumonia, type 2 diabetes, and neonatal disorders. Most deaths related to ambient and household air pollution are caused by human exposure to fine inhalable particles or fine particulate matter (PM), also known as $PM_{2.5}$ (Thurston el al., 2021; Ostro et al, 2021).[1] In 2019, about 6.4 million people died worldwide as a result of exposure to $PM_{2.5}$ air pollution, of which 4.1 million were due to $PM_{2.5}$ ambient air pollution and 2.3 million were due to $PM_{2.5}$ household air pollution from the use of solid fuels for cooking and other domestic purposes. Ninety-five percent of these deaths were in low- and middle-income countries (LMICs).

Understanding the welfare costs associated with air pollution has been a topic of continued attention. Several of these works have applied methodologies and estimates of exposure to air pollution used in the Global Burden of Disease (GBD) Project.[2] They all point to the enormous global welfare cost of air pollution in the trillions of dollars, equivalent in magnitude to 2.5–6 percent of global gross domestic product (GDP), depending on valuation of health damages (table 1.1). Some estimates indicate an upward trend in the global welfare cost of ambient air pollution. For example, the Organisation for Economic Co-operation and Development (OECD) estimates that the cost of health damages of ambient air pollution could increase to $20.5–$27.6 trillion (9–12 percent of GDP) by 2060 (OECD 2016).[3]

It is important to note the following two cost-related findings of these studies: (a) The global cost of ambient air pollution is substantially higher than the cost of household air pollution associated with the burning of solid fuels for cooking and other domestic purposes. (b) However, this report finds that the cost of household air pollution is still substantially higher than the cost of ambient air pollution in Sub-Saharan Africa and nearly as high as the cost of ambient air pollution in South Asia in 2019.

TABLE 1.1 **Global welfare cost of air pollution per year, trillions**

STUDY	DOMAIN	YEAR	$ (PPP)	US$	% OF GLOBAL GDP (PPP)	% OF GLOBAL GDP
Larsen (2014)	AAP	2012 in 2012 prices	–	1.7	–	2.5%
World Bank and IHME (2016)	AAP & HAP	2013 in 2011 prices	5.1	–	5.0%	–
OECD (2016)	AAP	2015 in 2010 prices	3.4	–		6.0%
Landrigan et al. (2018)	AAP & HAP	2015 in 2015 prices	–	3.8	–	5.1%[a]
World Bank (2020)	AAP	2016 in 2016 prices	5.7	3.3	4.8%	4.4%

Note: $ (PPP) = international dollars or purchasing power parity adjusted US$. GDP in PPP-adjusted US$ allows a comparison of the purchasing power of GDP of different countries. AAP = air pollution originating in the household environment; HAP = air pollution in the outdoor air.
a. Gross national income.

This report provides an updated estimate of the global, regional, and national cost of PM$_{2.5}$ air pollution in 2019 using the GBD 2019[4] estimates of mortality and morbidity from PM$_{2.5}$. The estimated global cost in 2019 was $8.1 trillion,[5] equivalent to 6.1 percent of global GDP (PPP adjusted).[6] In real terms, the estimated cost of PM$_{2.5}$ air pollution in 2019 is 40 percent higher than the estimate for 2013 in World Bank and IHME (2016).[7] The reasons for the higher cost estimate are mainly changes in exposure-response functions, the substantially higher estimate of global ambient PM$_{2.5}$ exposure, and the inclusion of an estimate of the cost of morbidity, as discussed below. The higher estimate of global ambient PM$_{2.5}$ is due more to improved methodology and availability of data than actual worsening of global ambient PM$_{2.5}$ air quality from 2013 to 2019, although the exact contribution of each of these two factors is difficult to ascertain.

This report also provides an overview of global and regional PM$_{2.5}$ population exposure and the exposure-response functions developed by the GBD 2019 study.

CONTEXT AND VALUE ADDED OF THIS REPORT

This report provides an estimate of the global, regional, and national costs of health damage—that is, of premature mortality and morbidity—from exposure to PM$_{2.5}$ air pollution in 2019. While recognizing the various costs of air pollution to society, this report focuses on estimating the cost of premature mortality and morbidity due to PM$_{2.5}$ ambient and household air pollution estimated by the GBD 2019 study. Estimating the health damage of air pollution in monetary terms provides a suitable metric for policy makers and decision-makers in developing countries to prioritize the design and implementation of policies and interventions for controlling PM$_{2.5}$ air pollution amid competing development challenges and budgetary and other resource constraints.

For the World Bank, as a development institution, the cost of PM$_{2.5}$ air pollution underscores the need for the Bank's sustained support of governments' efforts to reduce air pollution. Furthermore, the cost estimate provides a useful metric for informing decision-making and priority setting by governments in tackling the urgent problem of air pollution.

The value added of this report is as follows:

- The report is based on updated exposure-response functions as used by the GBD 2019 study. Exposure-response functions quantitatively relate the levels of $PM_{2.5}$ exposure to the risk of a health damage (COPD, stroke, IHD, lower respiratory infection, lung cancer, and type 2 diabetes).

- The GBD 2019 also incorporates $PM_{2.5}$ exposure-response functions for health outcomes that were not included in the GBD 2013, notably type 2 diabetes and neonatal disorders. Deaths from these additional health outcomes were over 10 percent of total deaths from $PM_{2.5}$ in 2019.

- This report is based on global ambient $PM_{2.5}$ exposure estimates used in the GBD 2019. These exposure estimates are higher than the estimates used in the GBD 2013 and are based on a database of ground-level measurements of air quality that is used for calibrating satellite and chemical transport modeling estimates of $PM_{2.5}$. The database of ground-level measurements used by the GBD 2019 is substantially larger than the database used in the GBD 2013 study. Global population-weighted ambient $PM_{2.5}$ exposure was 43 $\mu g/m^3$ in 2019 according to the estimates used in the GBD 2019 study, and 32 $\mu g/m^3$ in 2013 according to the GBD 2013 study.

- As a result of the changes in exposure-response functions and $PM_{2.5}$ exposure estimates from the GBD 2013 study to the GBD 2019 study, this report is based on a global mortality estimate of 6.4 million deaths from $PM_{2.5}$ in 2019 compared to 5.3 million deaths from $PM_{2.5}$ in 2013 used by the World Bank and IHME (2016).

- This report also provides an order-of-magnitude estimate of the cost of morbidity of $PM_{2.5}$ exposure based on the disease burden of morbidity reported by the GBD 2019 study, which is found to vary substantially across countries and regions.

The remaining sections of this report provide estimates of population exposure to $PM_{2.5}$, estimation of health damages from this exposure, the global costs of these health damages, and the policy implications underpinned by the report's findings.

NOTES

1. $PM_{2.5}$ is particulate matter (PM) with a diameter equal to or less than 2.5 micrometers, a diameter that is about 30 times smaller than that of a single human hair.
2. Several studies have been completed since the 1990s to estimate the Global Burden of Disease (GBD), originally commissioned by the World Bank to inform the preparation of *World Development Report 1993*. Comprehensive evaluations on ambient air pollution were also supported by WHO and the World Bank in 2000 and 2004. In the GBD 2010, the scope of the GBD was updated with support from the Bill & Melinda Gates Foundation to include 235 causes of death and disability from diseases and injuries, and 67 risk factors (including ambient air pollution) in 187 countries and territories in 21 regions of the world. The Institute for Health Metrics and Evaluation (IHME) became the main provider for a broad range of GBD estimates that underpinned the preparation of GBD Reports for 2010, 2013, 2015, 2016, 2017, and 2019. Most recently, the GBD 2019 included estimates of deaths and disability from 369 diseases and injuries, and 87 risk factors in 204 countries and territories (GBD 2019 Risk Factors Collaborators 2020).
3. 2010 Purchasing Power Parity (PPP) adjusted US$.
4. The GBD 2019 study is listed in the references sections of this report as GBD 2019 Risk Factors Collaborators (2020).
5. International dollars or purchasing power parity adjusted US$. Expressed in US dollars, the global cost in 2019 was US$4.4 trillion, equivalent to 5.1 percent of global GDP.
6. The cost equivalent to percent of GDP is the same whether expressed in GDP or PPP-adjusted GDP for each individual country, but not when aggregated globally.

7. The cost of PM$_{2.5}$ in 2013 was $5.11 trillion (in 2011 $ [PPP]) according to World Bank and IHME (2016). The cost in 2019 was $8.1 trillion, or $7.06 trillion in 2011 $ (PPP). The estimated cost in 2019 is therefore 40 percent higher than in 2013 in real terms.

REFERENCES

GBD 2013 Risk Factors Collaborators. 2015. "Global, Regional, and National Comparative Risk Assessment of 79 Behavioural, Environmental and Occupational, and Metabolic Risks or Clusters of Risks in 188 Countries, 1990–2013: A Systematic Analysis for the Global Burden of Disease Study 2013." *Lancet* 386: 2287–323.

GBD 2015 Risk Factors Collaborators. 2016. "Global, Regional, and National Comparative Risk Assessment of 79 Behavioural, Environmental and Occupational, and Metabolic Risks or Clusters of Risks, 1990–2015: A Systematic Analysis for the Global Burden of Disease Study 2015." *Lancet* 388: 1659–724.

GBD 2016 Risk Factors Collaborators. 2017. "Global, Regional, and National Comparative Risk Assessment of 84 Behavioural, Environmental and Occupational, and Metabolic Risks or Clusters of Risks, 1990–2016: A Systematic Analysis for the Global Burden of Disease Study 2016." *Lancet* 390: 1345–422.

GBD 2017 Risk Factors Collaborators. 2018. "Global, Regional, and National Comparative Risk Assessment of 84 Behavioural, Environmental and Occupational, and Metabolic Risks or Clusters of Risks for 195 Countries and Territories, 1990–2017: A Systematic Analysis for the Global Burden of Disease Study 2017." *Lancet* 392: 1923–94.

GBD 2019 Risk Factors Collaborators. 2020. "Global Burden of 87 Risk Factors in 204 Countries and Territories, 1990–2019: A Systematic Analysis for the Global Burden of Disease Study 2019." *Lancet* 396: 1223–49.

GBD 2019 Viewpoint Collaborators. 2020. "Five Insights from the Global Burden of Disease Study 2019." *Lancet* 396: 1135–59.

Landrigan, P. J., R. Fuller, N. J. R. Acosta, O. Adeyi, R. Arnold, N. N. Basu, A. B. Baldé, R. Bertollini, S. Bose-O'Reilly, J. I. Boufford, P. N. Breysse, T. Chiles, C. Mahidol, A. M. Coll-Seck, M. L. Cropper, J. Fobil, V. Fuster, M. Greenstone, A. Haines, D. Hanrahan, D. Hunter, M. Khare, A. Krupnick, B. Lanphear, B. Lohani, K. Martin, K. V. Mathiasen, M. A. McTeer, C. J. L. Murray, J. D. Ndahimananjara, F. Perera, J. Potočnik, A. S. Preker, J. Ramesh, J. Rockström, C. Salinas, L. D. Samson, K. Sandilya, P. D. Sly, K. R. Smith, A. Steiner, R. B. Stewart, W. A. Suk, O. C .P. van Schayck, G. N. Yadama, K. Yumkella, and M. Zhong. 2018. "The Lancet Commission on Pollution and Health." *Lancet* 391 (10119): 462–512.

Larsen, B. 2014. "Benefits and Costs of the Air Pollution Targets for the Post-2015 Development Agenda." Air Pollution Assessment Paper, Post-2015 Consensus Project. Copenhagen: Copenhagen Consensus Center. https://www.copenhagenconsensus.com/sites/default /files/air_pollution_assessment_-_larsen.pdf.

OECD (Organisation for Economic Co-operation and Development). 2016. *The Economic Consequences of Outdoor Air Pollution.* Paris: OECD.

Ostro, Bart; Yewande Awe; and Ernesto Sanchez-Triana. 2021. "When the Dust Settles: A Review of the Health Implications of the Dust Component of Air Pollution." World Bank, Washington, DC. https://openknowledge.worldbank.org/handle/10986/36267.

Thurston, George, Yewande Awe, Bart Ostro, and Ernesto Sanchez-Triana. 2021. *Are All Air Pollution Particles Equal? How Constituents and Sources of Fine Air Pollution Particles (PM$_{2.5}$) Affect Health.* A World Bank Study. Washington, DC: World Bank. https://openknowledge. worldbank.org/handle/10986/36269.

World Bank. 2020. *The Global Health Cost of Ambient PM$_{2.5}$ Air Pollution.* Washington, DC: World Bank. http://hdl.handle.net/10986/35721.

World Bank and IHME (Institute for Health Metrics and Evaluation). 2016. *The Cost of Air Pollution: Strengthening the Economic Case for Action.* Washington, DC: World Bank.

2 Evolution of Estimates of Population Exposure to PM$_{2.5}$

AMBIENT PM$_{2.5}$ EXPOSURE

The GBD studies estimate nationwide population exposure to ambient PM$_{2.5}$ from a combination of satellite imagery, chemical-transport modeling, and ground-level PM$_{2.5}$ and PM$_{10}$ measurements.

The evolution in satellite imagery/chemical transport model estimation techniques, the number of ground-level monitoring locations, and the method of calibrating the satellite imagery/chemical transport model estimates with the ground-level measurements has been quite substantial from the GBD 2010 study to the GBD 2019 study (Brauer et al. 2012, 2016; GBD 2019 Risk Factors Collaborators 2020; Shaddick et al. 2018; van Donkelaar et al. 2015, 2016).

Ground-level measurements of PM$_{2.5}$ or PM$_{10}$ employed by the GBD 2010 study covered fewer than 700 locations (Brauer et al. 2012). This expanded to 4,073 data points from 3,387 unique locations in the GBD 2013 study (Brauer et al. 2016). The GBD 2015 and GBD 2016 studies utilized the WHO Global Ambient Air Quality Database 2016 containing PM measurements from 6,003 ground monitors in about 3,000 human settlements (GBD 2015 Risk Factors Collaborators 2016; GBD 2016 Risk Factors Collaborators 2017; WHO 2016). The GBD 2017 utilized the WHO updated database 2018 with PM$_{10}$ and PM$_{2.5}$ from about 9,690 stations in nearly 4,400 locations (defined geographic areas) in 108 countries (GBD 2017 Risk Factors Collaborators 2018). The GBD 2019 also utilized this updated database, along with additional measurement data mainly from Bangladesh, Canada, China, the European Union, the United States, and PM measurement data from US embassies and consulates. Thus, measurement data from 10,408 ground monitors from 116 countries were utilized by the GBD 2019 (GBD 2019 Risk Factors Collaborators 2020). Nevertheless, ground monitoring remains particularly scarce in low-income countries and Sub-Saharan Africa.

PM$_{2.5}$ HOUSEHOLD AIR POLLUTION EXPOSURE

The GBD 2019 study estimates population exposure to PM$_{2.5}$ household air pollution from a combination of data on the percentage of countries' population using solid fuels for cooking and a household exposure prediction model.

The model is based on globally available measurement studies of PM$_{2.5}$ in the household environment, type of fuel used, and a sociodemographic index. The index is a composite of total fertility rate, education level, and income per capita, which all are considered important determinants of household air pollution exposure (GBD 2019 Risk Factors Collaborators 2020). This approach to exposure estimation represents a substantial improvement compared to simply using type of fuel—that is, percentage of the population using solid fuels—as a proxy for exposure, as was commonly done until less than a decade ago. Nevertheless, the number of measurement studies globally of personal exposure to PM$_{2.5}$ in the household environment is quite limited, and even more so for the male population and children (Shupler et al. 2018).

PM$_{2.5}$ POPULATION EXPOSURE

Global population annual exposure to ambient PM$_{2.5}$ was 43 µg/m^3 in 2019 according to estimates used by the GBD 2019 study. In contrast, the global population annual exposure in 2013 was 32 µg/m^3 according to estimates used by the GBD 2013 study. The difference is due more to changes in estimation methodology and increased availability of ground-level PM monitoring data reflected in the WHO database 2018 and other monitoring data used by the GBD 2019 study than to actual worsening of global ambient PM$_{2.5}$ air quality from 2013 to 2019, although the exact contribution of each of these two factors is difficult to ascertain. The changes in estimation methodology and availability of ground-level PM monitoring data are explained in the GBD 2019 study supplements (GBD 2019 Risk Factors Collaborators 2020).

The global ambient PM$_{2.5}$ population-exposure estimate for 2019 is over four times as high as WHO's Air Quality Guideline value of 10 µg/m^3 for annual average PM$_{2.5}$. Ambient PM$_{2.5}$ exposures in 2019 were highest in the South Asia (SA), Middle East and North Africa (MNA), and Sub-Saharan Africa (SSA) regions—that is, about 5–10 times as high as in North America (NA). PM$_{2.5}$ exposure is also high in East Asia and the Pacific (EAP), dominated by China at 48 µg/m^3 (figure 4.1, panel a).

Annual exposure to PM$_{2.5}$ is even higher among the population using solid fuels for cooking and other domestic purposes, with a global average of nearly 140 µg/m^3 for the population using traditional wood stoves (Shupler et al. 2018). The percentage of the population using solid fuels is highest in SSA (81 percent) and SA (61 percent) but also substantial in EAP (35 percent) and Latin America and the Caribbean (LAC) (13 percent) (figure 4.1, panel b).

REFERENCES

Brauer, M., M. Amann, R. T. Burnett, A. Cohen, F. Dentener, M. Ezzati, S. B. Henderson, M. Krzyzanowski, R. V. Martin, R. Van Dingenen, A. van Donkelaar, and G. D. Thurston. 2012. "Exposure Assessment for Estimation of the Global Burden of Disease Attributable to Outdoor Air Pollution." *Environ Sci Technol* 46 (2): 652–60.

Brauer, M., G. Freedman, J. Frostad, A. van Donkelaar, R. V. Martin, F. Dentener, R. van Dingenen, K. Estep, H. Amini, J. S. Apte, K. Balakrishnan, L. Barregard, D. Broday, V. Feigin, S. Ghosh, P. K. Hopke, L. D. Knibbs, Y. Kokubo, Y. Liu, S. Ma, L. Morawska, J. L. Sangrador, G. Shaddick, H. R. Anderson, T. Vos, M. H. Forouzanfar, R. T. Burnett, and A. Cohen. 2016. "Ambient Air

Pollution Exposure Estimation for the Global Burden of Disease 2013." *Environ Sci Technol* 50 (1): 79–88.

GBD 2013 Risk Factors Collaborators. 2015. "Global, Regional, and National Comparative Risk Assessment of 79 Behavioural, Environmental and Occupational, and Metabolic Risks or Clusters of Risks in 188 Countries, 1990–2013: A Systematic Analysis for the Global Burden of Disease Study 2013." *Lancet* 386: 2287–323.

GBD 2015 Risk Factors Collaborators. 2016. "Global, Regional, and National Comparative Risk Assessment of 79 Behavioural, Environmental and Occupational, and Metabolic Risks or Clusters of Risks, 1990–2015: A Systematic Analysis for the Global Burden of Disease Study 2015." *Lancet* 388: 1659–724.

GBD 2016 Risk Factors Collaborators. 2017. "Global, Regional, and National Comparative Risk Assessment of 84 Behavioural, Environmental and Occupational, and Metabolic Risks or Clusters of Risks, 1990–2016: A Systematic Analysis for the Global Burden of Disease Study 2016." *Lancet* 390: 1345–422.

GBD 2017 Risk Factors Collaborators. 2018. "Global, Regional, and National Comparative Risk Assessment of 84 Behavioural, Environmental and Occupational, and Metabolic Risks or Clusters of Risks for 195 Countries and Territories, 1990–2017: A Systematic Analysis for the Global Burden of Disease Study 2017." *Lancet* 392: 1923–94.

GBD 2019 Risk Factors Collaborators. 2020. "Global Burden of 87 Risk Factors in 204 Countries and Territories, 1990–2019: A Systematic Analysis for the Global Burden of Disease Study 2019." *Lancet* 396: 1223–49.

GBD 2019 Viewpoint Collaborators. 2020. "Five Insights from the Global Burden of Disease Study 2019." *Lancet* 396: 1135–59.

Shaddick, H. R. Anderson, T. Vos, M. H. Forouzanfar, R. T. Burnett, and A. Cohen. 2016. "Ambient Air Pollution Exposure Estimation for the Global Burden of Disease 2013." *Environ Sci Technol* 50 (1): 79–88.

Shaddick, G., M. I. Thomas, A. Green, M. Brauer, A. van Donkelaar, R. Burnett, H. Chang, A. Cohen, R. Van Dingenen, C. Dora, S. Gumy, Y. Liu, R. Martin, L. A. Waller, J. West, J. V. Zidek, and A. Prüss-Ustün. 2018. "Data Integration Model for Air Quality: A Hierarchical Approach to the Global Estimation of Exposures to Ambient Air Pollution." *Journal of the Royal Statistical Society. Series C, Applied Statistics 2018* 67: 231–53.

Shupler, M., W. Godwin, J. Frostad, P. Gustafson, R. E. Arku, and M. Brauer. 2018. "Global Estimation of Exposure to Fine Particulate Matter (PM~2.5~) from Household Air Pollution." *Environment International* 120: 354–63.

Van Donkelaar, A., R. Martin, M. Brauer, and B. Boys. 2015. "Use of Satellite Observations for Long-Term Exposure Assessment of Global Concentrations of Fine Particulate Matter." *Environmental Health Perspectives* 123: 135–43.

Van Donkelaar, A., R. V. Martin, M. Brauer, N. C. Hsu, R.A. Kahn, R. C. Levy, A. Lyapustin, A. M. Sayer, and D. M. Winker. 2016. "Global Estimates of Fine Particulate Matter Using a Combined Geophysical-Statistical Method with Information from Satellites, Models, and Monitors." *Environmental Science and Technology* 50: 3762–72.

WHO (World Health Organization). 2016. *Ambient Air Pollution: A Global Assessment of Exposure and Burden of Disease.* Geneva: WHO.

3 Risks of Health Damages from PM$_{2.5}$ Exposure

Exposure-response functions or concentration-response functions are a key input for quantifying the health burden of air pollution. One such function is the Integrated Exposure-Response (IER) function, so called because it integrates exposures to PM$_{2.5}$ from different sources. The GBD 2019 project estimates health damages of PM$_{2.5}$ exposure from IER functions for six major health outcomes, as well as using a somewhat different approach to estimating neonatal disorders. The GBD project first developed IER functions for the GBD 2010 study (see appendix B). These IER functions provide the relative risks of health damages of PM$_{2.5}$ at exposures ranging from less than 5 µg/m³ to several hundred µg/m³. Thus, the risk functions can be applied to a wide range of ambient PM$_{2.5}$ concentrations found around the world as well as to high household air-pollution levels of PM$_{2.5}$ from combustion of solid fuels.

The relative risks from the IER function used by the GBD 2019 study are published in the GBD 2019 study Supplement (GBD 2019 Risk Factors Collaborators 2020).

They are reproduced in figure 3.1 for PM$_{2.5}$ concentrations up to 200 µg/m³.[1]

The relative risks rise very steeply to 35 µg/m³. The relative risk of type 2 diabetes then flattens out with minimal additional risk at higher exposure levels. The relative risks of IHD, lung cancer, and stroke flatten out from 90 µg/m³.[2] The relative risks of lower respiratory infections (LRI) and chronic obstructively pulmonary disease (COPD) continue to rise with higher exposure levels.

The rise in relative risks (up to a PM$_{2.5}$ exposure level of about 90 µg/m³ for five of the six health outcomes) means an increasing burden of health effects over the range of national population-weighted ambient PM$_{2.5}$ globally.[3] The flattening of the relative risks for four of the six health outcomes also means that the health benefits of reducing PM$_{2.5}$ exposures (from, for instance, 200 µg/m³ to 90 µg/m³) are very modest and mostly related to COPD and LRI.

FIGURE 3.1

Relative risks of major health outcomes associated with PM$_{2.5}$ exposure, GBD 2019 study

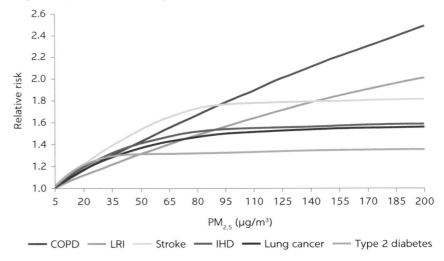

Source: Based on the GBD 2019 study supplement (GBD 2019 Risk Factors Collaborators 2020).
Note: The relative risks (RR) presented here are relative to the risks at a theoretical minimum-risk exposure level (TMREL). A TMREL of 4μg/m3 has been applied. RR = RR(X)/RR(TMREL) where X is PM2.5 exposure in μg/m3. COPD = chronic obstructive pulmonary disease, IHD = ischemic heart disease, LC = lung cancer; LRI = lower respiratory infections. The relative risk for IHD and strokes are age-weighted averages.

This has important implications for how to combat the health effects of PM$_{2.5}$ household air pollution from the use of traditional cookstoves with solid fuels in low- and middle-income countries (LMICs). Improved cookstoves, often 40–60 percent more energy efficient than traditional stoves, have been found to reduce exposure by around 50 percent. However, this exposure reduction (from, for instance, 200 to 100 μg/m³ or 140 to 70 μg/m³) reduces health effects by as little as 11–12 percent, based on analysis of the IER functions from the GBD 2019. Therefore, effectively combating the health effects requires clean cooking fuels and technologies, such as LPG or electricity. Some LMICs have already achieved a high prevalence rate of the population using clean fuels and technologies, demonstrating this possibility even at moderate GDP per capita levels.

The GBD 2019 exposure-response functions differ in important aspects from the exposure-response functions from the GBD 2016 and 2017 studies. The differences are presented in figure 3.2 for 45 μg/m³ and 140 μg/m³ of annual PM$_{2.5}$ exposure. These exposure levels correspond closely to the global average ambient PM$_{2.5}$ exposure in 2019 and the global average household air pollution PM$_{2.5}$ exposure level among populations using traditional wood stoves for cooking and other domestic purposes. The GBD 2019 exposure-response functions reveal much higher relative risk of stroke and IHD and lower relative risk of LRI for both PM$_{2.5}$ exposure levels than the GBD 2016 and GBD 2017 functions. The relative risk of COPD is similar for the three GBD editions at 45 μg/m³ but substantially higher in the GBD 2019 than in GBD 2016 and GBD 2017. The relative risk of lung cancer is higher in the GBD 2019 at 45 μg/m³ but lower at 140 μg/m³ than in the GBD 2016 and GBD 2017.

FIGURE 3.2

Relative risks of major health outcomes associated with PM$_{2.5}$ exposure, GBD 2016–19

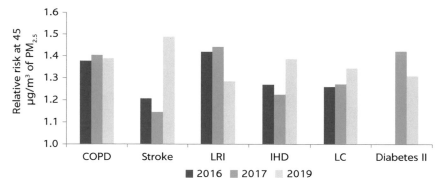

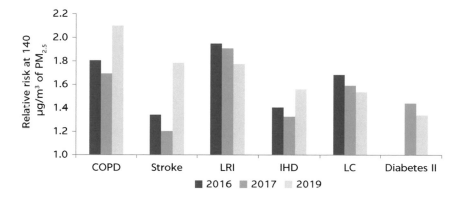

Source: From the GBD 2016, 2017, and 2019 studies.
Note: COPD = chronic obstructive pulmonary disease, IHD = ischemic heart disease, LC = lung cancer; LRI = lower respiratory infections. The relative risk for IHD and stroke are age-weighted averages.

GLOBAL HEALTH DAMAGES OF PM$_{2.5}$ EXPOSURE

As many as 6.45 million people died from PM$_{2.5}$ ambient and household air pollution in 2019 according to the GBD 2019 study. This makes PM$_{2.5}$ exposure the fifth-largest health risk factor of global deaths after high blood pressure, dietary risks, tobacco smoking, and diabetes, among dozens of risk factors assessed by the GBD 2019 study. However, PM$_{2.5}$ is the largest health risk factor in LI countries, the second-largest in LMI countries, and the fourth-largest in UMI countries.

Nearly two-thirds of global deaths from PM$_{2.5}$ exposure was from ambient air pollution (4.14 million) and nearly one-third from household air pollution (2.31 million). As many as 95 percent of deaths from PM$_{2.5}$ exposure occurred in low- and middle-income countries. A comparison of the risks considered in the GBD 2019 study shows that exposure to ambient air pollution increased at an annualized rate of change of 1.47 between 2010 and 2019, the second highest during this period, only after high body-mass index (GBD 2019 Viewpoint Collaborators 2020).

Globally, IHD and stroke account for 53 percent of deaths from PM$_{2.5}$; respiratory illnesses for 35 percent including COPD, LRI, and lung cancer;

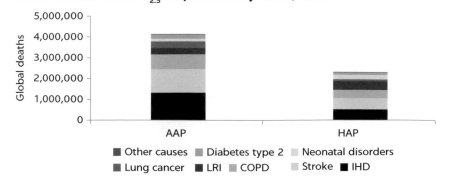

FIGURE 3.3A

Global deaths from PM$_{2.5}$ air pollution by cause, 2019

Source: Based on data from IHME, GBD 2019 study.
Note: AAP = ambient air pollution; HAP = household air pollution; COPD = chronic obstructive pulmonary disease; IHD = ischemic heart disease; LC = lung cancer; LRI = lower respiratory infections.

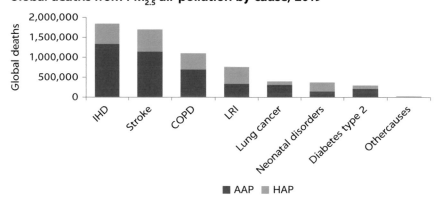

FIGURE 3.3B

Global deaths from PM$_{2.5}$ air pollution by cause, 2019

Source: Based on data from IHME, GBD 2019 study.
Note: AAP = ambient air pollution; HAP = household air pollution; COPD = chronic obstructive pulmonary disease; IHD = ischemic heart disease; LC = lung cancer; LRI = lower respiratory infections.

neonatal disorders for 6 percent; diabetes for 5 percent; and other diseases for less than 1 percent according to the GBD 2019 study (figures 3.3a, 3.3b, 3.4).

In perspective, global deaths from PM$_{2.5}$ air pollution constituted as much as 11.4 percent of all global deaths in 2019. For the main health outcomes, PM$_{2.5}$ exposure caused as much as 30–33 percent of global deaths from COPD and LRI; 20–26 percent of global deaths from IHD and stroke; and 19–20 percent of global deaths from lung cancer, neonatal disorders, and type 2 diabetes (figure 3.5).

Seventy percent of global deaths from PM$_{2.5}$ air pollution in 2019 occurred in EAP and SA (figure 3.6). China accounted for 74 percent of the deaths in EAP, and India accounted for 76 percent in SA. Deaths from PM$_{2.5}$ in these two countries constituted 52 percent of global deaths from PM$_{2.5}$.

The three (and for one region, the two) countries with the most deaths from PM$_{2.5}$ air pollution in each region in 2019 are presented in table 3.1. There are six countries with more than 100,000 deaths from PM$_{2.5}$, and nine countries with 50,000–100,000 deaths, three of which are not in table 3.1.

Eighty-five percent of global deaths from PM$_{2.5}$ air pollution occurred in middle-income countries, nearly evenly split between lower-middle-income and

FIGURE 3.4

Share of global deaths from PM$_{2.5}$: Ambient and household air pollution by cause, 2019

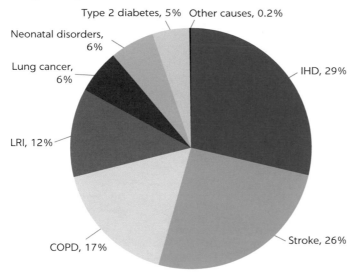

Source: Based on data from IHME, GBD 2019 study.
Note: AAP = ambient air pollution; HAP = household air pollution; COPD = chronic obstructive pulmonary disease; IHD = ischemic heart disease; LC = lung cancer; LRI = lower respiratory infections.

FIGURE 3.5

Global deaths by cause from PM$_{2.5}$ air pollution as a share of all global deaths, 2019

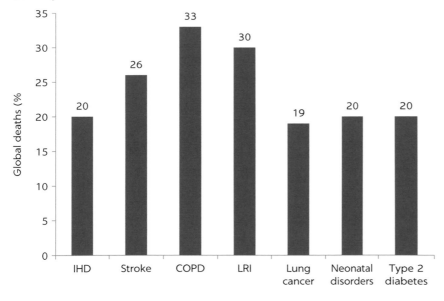

Source: Based on data from IHME, GBD 2019 study.
Note: COPD = chronic obstructive pulmonary disease; IHD = ischemic heart disease; LRI = lower respiratory infections. EAP = East Asia and Pacific; SA = South Asia; SSA = Sub-Saharan Africa; ECA = Europe and Central Asia; MNA = Middle East and North Africa; LAC = Latin America and Caribbean; NA = North America.

upper-middle-income. Ten percent of deaths were in low-income countries and 5 percent in high-income countries (figure 3.7).

Not only are the majority of deaths from PM$_{2.5}$ air pollution in EAP and SA, but these regions also have the highest death rates from PM$_{2.5}$, reaching 103 and 111 deaths per 100,000 population, respectively. This is 7–8 times higher than in NA (figure 3.8).

FIGURE 3.6

Global number of deaths from PM$_{2.5}$ exposure by region, 2019

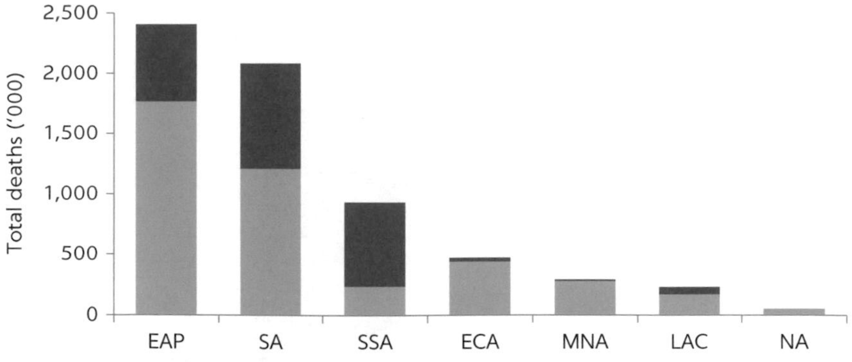

	EAP	SA	SSA	ECA	MNA	LAC	NA
■ HAP	641	876	695	31	12	59	0
■ AAP	1,767	1,205	234	437	276	169	52

Source: Based on data from IHME, GBD 2019 study.
Note: AAP = ambient air pollution; HAP = household air pollution; EAP = East Asia and Pacific; SA = South Asia; SSA = Sub-Saharan Africa; ECA = Europe and Central Asia; MNA = Middle East and North Africa; LAC = Latin America and Caribbean; NA = North America.

TABLE 3.1 **Number of deaths from PM$_{2.5}$ exposure by region and country, 2019 ('000)**

REGION	COUNTRY	DEATHS	REGION	COUNTRY	DEATHS
EAP	China	1,787	NA	United States	48
	Indonesia	184		Canada	4
	Philippines	75	SA	India	1,587
ECA	Russian Federation	76		Pakistan	230
	Ukraine	46		Bangladesh	169
	Turkey	42	SSA	Nigeria	197
LAC	Brazil	58		Ethiopia	77
	Mexico	46		Congo, Dem. Rep.	69
	Colombia	15			
MNA	Egypt, Arab Rep.	91			
	Iran, Islamic Rep.	42			
	Morocco	29			

Source: Based on data from IHME, GBD 2019 study.
Note: EAP = East Asia and Pacific; ECA = Europe and Central Asia; LAC = Latin America and Caribbean; MNA = Middle East and North Africa; NA = North America; SA = South Asia; SSA = Sub-Saharan Africa.

By income group, the highest death rates from PM$_{2.5}$ exposure are in lower-middle-income countries, and lowest in the high-income OECD countries (figure 3.9).

The three (and in one region, the two) countries in each region with the highest death rates from PM$_{2.5}$ air pollution are presented in table 3.2. The countries with the highest death rates are in EAP, ECA, SA, and SSA, reaching 106–202 deaths per 100,000 population. There are 32 countries with death rates over 100 per 100,000 population. Thirty-one of the countries are in these four regions, and one is in LAC.

Globally, deaths from PM$_{2.5}$ air pollution constituted 11.4 percent of all deaths from all causes in 2019. The death rate reaches as high as 17 percent in SA, or ten

FIGURE 3.7

Global number of deaths from PM$_{2.5}$ exposure by income group, 2019

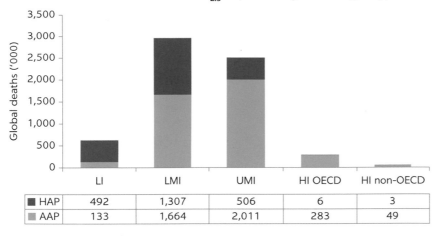

	LI	LMI	UMI	HI OECD	HI non-OECD
■ HAP	492	1,307	506	6	3
■ AAP	133	1,664	2,011	283	49

Source: Based on data from IHME, GBD 2019 study.
Note: AAP = ambient air pollution; HAP = household air pollution; LI = low-income countries; LMI = lower-middle-income countries; UMI = upper-middle-income countries; and HI = high-income countries. Assignment of countries to categories based on World Bank income classification.

FIGURE 3.8

Number of deaths from PM$_{2.5}$ exposure per 100,000 population in 2019, by region

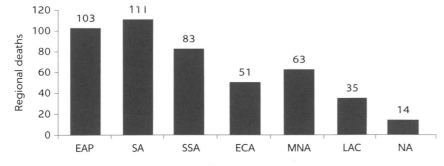

Source: Based on data from IHME, GBD 2019 study.
Note: EAP = East Asia and Pacific; SA = South Asia; SSA= Sub-Saharan Africa; ECA = Europe and Central Asia; MNA = Middle East and North Africa; LAC = Latin America and Caribbean; NA = North America.

FIGURE 3.9

Number of deaths from PM$_{2.5}$ exposure per 100,000 population in 2019, by income group

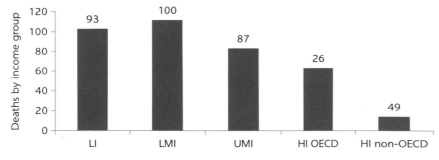

Source: Based on data from IHME, GBD 2019 study.
Note: LI = low-income countries; LMI = lower-middle-income countries; UMI = upper-middle-income countries; and HI = high-income countries. Assignment of countries to categories based on World Bank income classification.

TABLE 3.2 **Number of deaths from PM$_{2.5}$ exposure per 100,000 population, by country, 2019**

REGION	COUNTRY	DEATH RATE	REGION	COUNTRY	DEATH RATE
EAP	Korea, Dem. People's Rep.	202	NA	United States	15
	Myanmar	134		Canada	10
	China	126	SA	Nepal	130
ECA	Bulgaria	157		India	114
	North Macedonia	153		Bangladesh	106
	Bosnia and Herzegovina	145	SSA	Central African Republic	149
LAC	Haiti	113		Somalia	139
	Trinidad and Tobago	64		Chad	132
	Guyana	60			
MNA	Egypt, Arab Rep.	91			
	Morocco	80			
	Syria	72			

Source: Based on data from IHME, GBD 2019 study.
Note: EAP = East Asia and Pacific; ECA = Europe and Central Asia; LAC = Latin America and Caribbean; MNA = Middle East and North Africa, NA = North America; SA = South Asia; SSA = Sub-Saharan Africa.

TABLE 3.3 **Deaths from PM$_{2.5}$ exposure as a share of all deaths by region, 2019**

REGION	COUNTRY	DEATH RATE	REGION	COUNTRY	DEATH RATE
EAP	Korea, Dem. People's Rep.	22%	NA	United States	1.6%
	Papua New Guinea	18%		Canada	1.3%
	Myanmar	17%	SA	Nepal	20%
ECA	Tajikistan	15%		Bangladesh	20%
	Uzbekistan	15%		India	17%
	North Macedonia	14%	SSA	Somalia	15%
LAC	Haiti	14%		Gambia, The	15%
	Honduras	11%		Niger	15%
	Guatemala	10%			
MNA	Egypt, Arab Rep.	16%			
	Kuwait	15%			
	Bahrain	15%			

Source: Based on data from IHME, GBD 2019 study.
Note: EAP = East Asia and Pacific; SA= South Asia; SSA= Sub-Saharan Africa; ECA = Europe and Central Asia; MNA = Middle East and North Africa; LAC = Latin America and Caribbean; NA = North America.

times higher than in NA. By income group, the death rate reaches 14–15 percent in low-income and lower middle-income countries, compared to 2.8 percent in high-income OECD countries (table 3.3, figure 3.10).

The three (and in one region, the two) countries in each region with the highest death rates—that is, number of deaths from PM$_{2.5}$ as a percentage of all deaths from all causes—are presented in table 3.4. The countries with the highest death rates are in EAP and SA, followed by ECA, MNA, and SSA. There are 17 countries in which deaths from PM$_{2.5}$ exceed 15 percent of total deaths. Thirteen of these countries are in EAP and SA.

FIGURE 3.10

Deaths from PM$_{2.5}$ exposure as a share of all deaths by income group, 2019

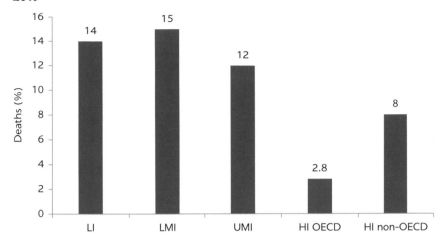

Source: Based on data from IHME, GBD 2019 study.
Note: LI = low-income countries; LMI = lower-middle-income countries; UMI = upper-middle-income countries; and HI = high-income countries. Classification according to World Bank income taxonomy.

TABLE 3.4 **Deaths from PM$_{2.5}$ exposure as a share of all deaths by country, 2019**

REGION	COUNTRY	DEATH RATE	REGION	COUNTRY	DEATH RATE
EAP	Korea, Dem. People's Rep.	22%	NA	United States	1.6%
	Papua New Guinea	18%		Canada	1.3%
	Myanmar	17%	SA	Nepal	20%
ECA	Tajikistan	15%		Bangladesh	20%
	Uzbekistan	15%		India	17%
	North Macedonia	14%	SSA	Somalia	15%
LAC	Haiti	14%		Gambia, The	15%
	Honduras	11%		Niger	15%
	Guatemala	10%			
MNA	Egypt, Arab Rep.	16%			
	Kuwait	15%			
	Bahrain	15%			

Source: Based on data from IHME, GBD 2019 study.
Note: EAP = East Asia and Pacific; ECA = Europe and Central Asia; LAC = Latin America and Caribbean; MNA = Middle East and North Africa, NA = North America; SA = South Asia; SSA = Sub-Saharan Africa.

The GBD 2019 study also estimates that PM$_{2.5}$ air pollution caused morbidity in the magnitude of 22.2 million years lived with disability (YLDs) in 2019, or about 3.3 YLDs per death from PM$_{2.5}$. About 13.3 million YLDs were from ambient PM$_{2.5}$ and 7.9 million from PM$_{2.5}$ household air pollution. As many as 82 percent of the YLDs were type 2 diabetes, COPD, and stroke (figures 3.11, 3.12).

The YLDs from PM$_{2.5}$ exposure are equivalent to 93 billion days lived with illness (table 3.4). The 93 billion days' total is based on the following

FIGURE 3.11

Global YLDs from PM$_{2.5}$ air pollution by cause, 2019

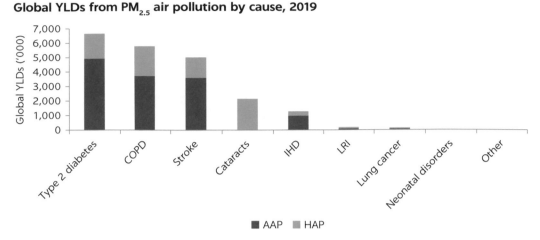

■ AAP   ■ HAP

Source: Based on data from IHME, GBD 2019 study.
Note: YLD = years lived with disability; AAP = ambient air pollution; HAP = household air pollution; COPD = chronic obstructive pulmonary disease, IHD = ischemic heart disease, LRI = lower respiratory infections.

FIGURE 3.12

Share of global YLDs from PM$_{2.5}$ air pollution by cause, 2019

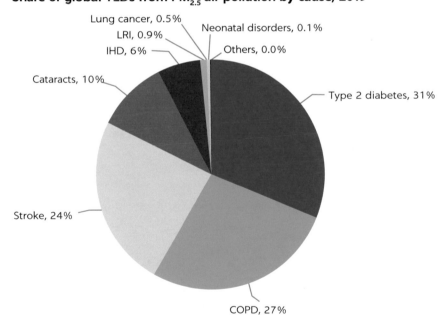

Source: Based on data from IHME, GBD 2019 study.
Note: YLD = years lived with disability; COPD = chronic obstructive pulmonary disease, IHD = ischemic heart disease, LRI = lower respiratory infections.

formula: days lived with illness = (YLDs x 365) / disability weight of disease, with disability weight ranging from 0 to 1. This very large number is due to the fact that many individuals contracting many of the diseases associated with PM$_{2.5}$ exposure live with the diseases for many years. These include type 2 diabetes, COPD, stroke, cataracts, and IHD.

GLOBAL COST OF PM$_{2.5}$ EXPOSURE

The health damages of PM$_{2.5}$ air pollution can be monetized to provide an estimate of the welfare cost of PM$_{2.5}$. Valuation of mortality in this report follows the welfare approach or value of statistical life (VSL) in World Bank and IHME (2016) (see appendix C). Valuation of morbidity, measured as the cost of days of illness, is valued at a fraction of wage rates (see appendix D).

The global cost of health damages from PM$_{2.5}$ air pollution was $8.1 trillion in 2019, equivalent to 6.1 percent of global GDP (PPP adjusted).

The cost of ambient PM$_{2.5}$ was $6.43 trillion, equivalent to 4.8 percent of global GDP (PPP adjusted), and the cost of PM$_{2.5}$ household air pollution was $1.67 trillion, equivalent to 1.3 percent of global GDP (PPP adjusted).

The estimated cost of PM$_{2.5}$ air pollution in 2019 is 40 percent higher in real terms than the estimate for 2013 in World Bank and IHME (2016). The reasons for the higher cost estimate are mainly changes in exposure-response functions, substantially higher estimate of global ambient PM$_{2.5}$ exposure, and inclusion of an estimate of the cost of morbidity. The higher estimate of global ambient PM$_{2.5}$ exposure is more due to improved methodology and availability of ground-level PM monitoring data than actual worsening of global ambient PM$_{2.5}$ air quality from 2013 to 2019, although the exact contribution of each of these two factors is difficult to ascertain.

About 85 percent of the total global cost of health damages in 2019 is from premature mortality and 15 percent from morbidity. Cost of morbidity as a share of total cost of health damages by country varies from as low as 4 percent to as high as 33 percent across countries. The overall global cost of morbidity, relative to the cost of mortality, is very similar to the estimate by the OECD in its report on the global economic consequences of outdoor air pollution (OECD 2016) (see appendix D).

The cost of health damages from PM$_{2.5}$ air pollution was highest in SA and EAP, at equivalents of 10.3 and 9.3 percent of GDP (PPP adjusted), respectively. The cost of PM$_{2.5}$ household air pollution constituted a substantial share of total cost in SA and SSA; a moderate share in EAP and LAC; and a small share in MNA, ECA, and NA. Cost of mortality dominated total cost in all regions. The morbidity cost share ranged from 13 percent to 15 percent in EAP, ECA, LAC, MNA, and SSA; to 20 percent in SA; and to 22 percent in NA (figure 3.13).

By income group, the cost of PM$_{2.5}$ air pollution was equivalent to 8.9 percent of GDP (PPP adjusted) in low- and middle-income countries, and 3.0 percent in high-income countries. The cost peaked at 9.1 percent in UMI countries and 9.0 percent in LMI countries. The cost of PM$_{2.5}$ household air pollution was a dominant share in LI countries, a substantial share in LMI countries, and a moderate share in UMI countries. The cost of PM$_{2.5}$ air pollution was lowest in high-income OECD countries, equivalent to 2.8 percent of GDP (PPP adjusted) (figure 3.14).

The three (and for one region, the two) countries in each region with the highest welfare cost of PM$_{2.5}$ air pollution as a percentage of GDP are presented in table 3.5. The countries with the highest costs are in ECA, followed by EAP and SA. There are 17 countries in which the welfare cost of PM$_{2.5}$ exceeds the equivalent of 10 percent of GDP. Fifteen of these countries are in ECA and EAP, and two are in SA. The reason for the high cost in many ECA countries is largely associated with the high baseline death rates in many ECA countries. Costs by country are presented in appendix A.

FIGURE 3.13

Annual cost of health damage from PM$_{2.5}$ exposure by region, percent equivalent of GDP (PPP), 2019

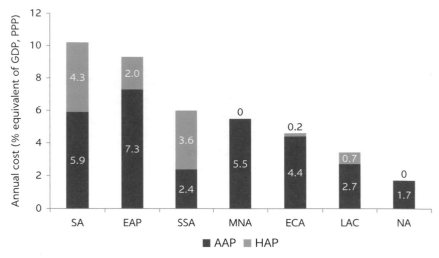

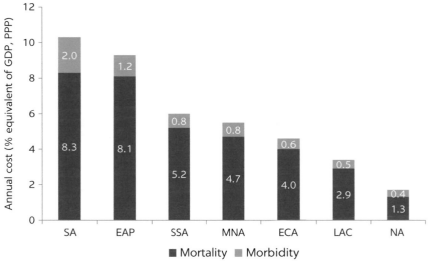

Source: Original calculations for this publication.
Note: Numbers may not add up due to rounding. AAP = ambient air pollution; HAP = household air pollution; EAP = East Asia and Pacific; ECA = Europe and Central Asia; LAC = Latin America and Caribbean; MNA = Middle East and North Africa, NA = North America; SA = South Asia; SSA = Sub-Saharan Africa.

The cost of PM$_{2.5}$ air pollution estimated in this report for the year 2019, along with cost estimates in previous reports for previous years, cannot readily be compared to infer whether global air quality has worsened or improved. This is mainly because each cost estimate is based on (a) exposure-response functions that are evolving over time as new evidence becomes available; (b) global ambient PM$_{2.5}$ population-exposure estimates that also evolve over time with methodological developments and increased availability of ground-level PM monitoring data; and (c) modifications in the valuation in health damages (that is, the inclusion of cost of morbidity in this report). Each cost estimate should rather be viewed as a reflection of available evidence and scientific understanding at the time of the estimate. The global burden, in YLDs and days lived with disease, of morbidity from PM$_{2.5}$ exposure is presented in table 3.6.

FIGURE 3.14

Annual cost of health damage from PM$_{2.5}$ exposure by income group, percent equivalent of GDP (PPP), 2019

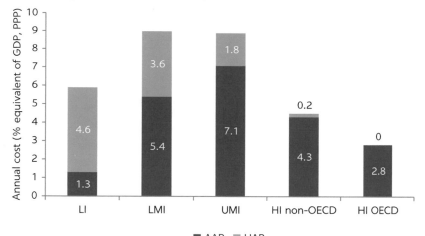

AAP ■ HAP

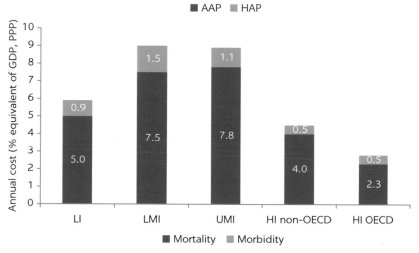

■ Mortality ■ Morbidity

Source: Original calculations for this publication.
Note: AAP = ambient air pollution; HAP = household air pollution; LI = low-income countries; LMI = lower-middle-income countries; UMI = upper-middle-income countries; and HI = high-income countries. Assignment of countries to categories based on World Bank income classification.

TABLE 3.5 **Annual cost of health damages from PM$_{2.5}$ by country, percent equivalent of GDP, 2019**

REGION	COUNTRY	COST	REGION	COUNTRY	COST
EAP	China	12.9%	NA	United States	1.7%
	Papua New Guinea	12.0%		Canada	1.2%
	Myanmar	11.4%	SA	India	10.6%
ECA	Serbia	18.9%		Nepal	10.2%
	Bulgaria	16.3%		Pakistan	8.9%
	North Macedonia	15.9%	SSA	Burkina Faso	9.1%
LAC	Barbados	8.8%		Mali	9.1%
	Haiti	8.1%		Central African Republic	8.7%
	Trinidad and Tobago	7.8%			
MNA	Egypt, Arab Rep.	8.6%			
	Morocco	7.3%			
	Tunisia	6.5%			

Source: Original calculations for this publication.
Note: EAP = East Asia and Pacific; ECA = Europe and Central Asia; LAC = Latin America and Caribbean; MNA = Middle East and North Africa, NA = North America; SA = South Asia; SSA = Sub-Saharan Africa.

TABLE 3.6 **Global burden of morbidity from PM$_{2.5}$ exposure, 2019**

DISEASE	YLDs	DAYS LIVED WITH DISEASE (MILLION)
Type 2 diabetes	6,653,020	30,252
COPD	5,830,818	22,780
Stroke	5,028,001	10,497
Cataracts	2,143,472	11,370
IHD	1,248,232	16,654
LRI	198,029	1,214
Lung cancer	99,225	214
Neonatal disorders	19,482	35
Other	8,415	
Total	21,228,694	93,016

Source: Based on data from IHME, GBD 2019 study.
Note: YLD = years lived with disability; COPD = chronic obstructive pulmonary disease, IHD = ischemic heart disease, LRI = lower respiratory infections.

NOTES

1. Relative risks are available at http://ghdx.healthdata.org/record/ihme-data/global-burden-disease-study-2019-gbd-2019-particulate-matter-risk-curves.
2. Relative risks for IHD and stroke are population age-weighted and vary across countries in relation to the age structure of IHD and stroke mortality.
3. The highest national population-weighted ambient PM$_{2.5}$ in 2019 was 83 µg/m³ according to the GBD 2019 (HEI 2020).

REFERENCES

GBD 2016 Risk Factors Collaborators. 2017. "Global, Regional, and National Comparative Risk Assessment of 84 Behavioural, Environmental and Occupational, and Metabolic Risks or Clusters of Risks, 1990–2016: A Systematic Analysis for the Global Burden of Disease Study 2016." *Lancet* 390: 1345–422.

GBD 2017 Risk Factors Collaborators. 2018. "Global, Regional, and National Comparative Risk Assessment of 84 Behavioural, Environmental and Occupational, and Metabolic Risks or Clusters of Risks for 195 Countries and Territories, 1990–2017: A Systematic Analysis for the Global Burden of Disease Study 2017." *Lancet* 392: 1923–94.

GBD 2019 Risk Factors Collaborators. 2020. "Global Burden of 87 Risk Factors in 204 Countries and Territories, 1990–2019: A Systematic Analysis for the Global Burden of Disease Study 2019." *Lancet* 396: 1223–49.

GBD 2019 Viewpoint Collaborators. 2020. "Five Insights from the Global Burden of Disease Study 2019." *Lancet* 396: 1135–59.

HEI (Health Effects Institute). 2020. *State of Global Air 2020.* Boston: HEI. www.stateofglobalair.org.

OECD (Organisation for Economic Co-operation and Development). 2016. *The Economic Consequences of Outdoor Air Pollution.* Paris: OECD.

World Bank and IHME (Institute for Health Metrics and Evaluation). 2016. *The Cost of Air Pollution: Strengthening the Economic Case for Action.* Washington, DC: World Bank.

4 Outlook and Policy Implications

This report provides an estimate of the global cost of $PM_{2.5}$ ambient and household air pollution in 2019 based on the GBD 2019 study. It thus represents an update of the estimated cost in 2013 reported in World Bank and IHME (2016) that was based on the GBD 2013 study.

This report distinguishes itself from the 2013 estimate in important aspects. It is based on

- Revised exposure-response functions from the GBD 2019 study that differ from the functions from the GBD 2013 study for several health outcomes;
- Revised global ambient $PM_{2.5}$ population-exposure estimates from the GBD 2019 study that are based on calibration from a substantially larger database of PM ground-level measurements than the data used for the GBD 2013 study; and
- Inclusion of an estimate of the cost of morbidity based on estimates of years living with disease from $PM_{2.5}$ air pollution reported by the GBD 2019 study.

Health damages and costs of $PM_{2.5}$ air pollution are staggering, especially in developing countries, globally reaching 6.4 million deaths and 93 billion days lived with illness in 2019, with a welfare cost of $8.1 trillion, equivalent to 6.1 percent of global GDP (PPP adjusted).

This estimated cost for 2019 is 40 percent higher in real terms than the estimate for 2013 in World Bank and IHME (2016). The reasons for the higher cost estimate are mainly changes in exposure-response functions, substantially higher estimate of global ambient $PM_{2.5}$ exposure due to improved methodology and ground-level PM monitoring data availability, and inclusion of an estimate of the cost of morbidity. The higher estimate of global ambient $PM_{2.5}$ exposure is more due to improved methodology and availability of ground-level PM monitoring data than actual worsening of global ambient $PM_{2.5}$ air quality from 2013 to 2019, although the exact contribution of each of these two factors is difficult to ascertain.

About 85 percent of the total global cost of health damages in 2019 is from premature mortality and 15 percent from morbidity. Cost of morbidity as a share of total cost varies from as low as 4 percent to as high as 33 percent across countries.

Seventy percent of the health damages occur in the SA and EAP regions.

Costs reach as high as 10.6 to 12.9 percent of GDP in China and India, the two countries in which over half of global deaths from PM$_{2.5}$ air pollution occur.

The methodology and ground-level measurement data available for the global ambient PM$_{2.5}$ population-exposure estimates from the GBD 2019 study represent important improvements over the estimates from the GBD 2013 study, based on calibration from a larger PM ground-level measurement database. However, the database nevertheless contains PM measurements from only a little over half of the countries in the world and is almost entirely lacking from large parts of SSA.

PM$_{2.5}$ measurements are particularly scarce in low-income countries and SSA, with one monitor per 65 and 28 million people, respectively, in contrast to one monitor per 0.37 million people in high-income countries.

The estimates provided in this report indicate that PM$_{2.5}$ air pollution causes significant health and economic burdens. These burdens are particularly significant in low- and middle-income countries, and in regions such as South Asia and East Asia and Pacific. Even though the costs presented in this report are equivalent to a sizable share of national and regional GDPs, they should be considered as conservative estimates because they do not consider several health effects of air pollution that are still the subject of research, such as mental health conditions or neurological impairment. The estimates also do not include other economic and environmental impacts of air pollution, including aesthetic impacts, loss of agricultural productivity, or its contributions to climate change.

Since 2016, the World Health Organization (WHO) has been reviewing the growing body of scientific research assessing the health effects of air pollution. The reviews that have been published to date point at robust evidence of negative health effects of short- and long-term exposure to air pollutants, even at levels that were previously considered safe, including

- Long-term exposure to particulate matter pollution, particularly PM$_{2.5}$, is clearly associated with increased mortality from all causes, cardiovascular disease, respiratory disease, and lung cancer, even at exposure levels below the current WHO guideline annual exposure level of 10 μg/m^3 for PM$_{2.5}$ (Chen and Hoek 2020).
- There is strong evidence showing a robust, positive association between short-term exposure to PM$_{10}$, PM$_{2.5}$, NO$_2$, and O$_3$ and all-cause mortality, and between PM$_{10}$ and PM$_{2.5}$ and cardiovascular, respiratory, and cerebrovascular mortality (Orellano et al. 2020).
- Short-term exposure to sulfur dioxide (SO$_2$), ranging from increases in exposure from one hour to a 24-hour average, is robustly associated with increased mortality (Orellano, Reynoso, and Quaranta 2021)

AREAS FOR ACTION

As scientific research continues to evolve, there is a high probability that evidence will show that the health and economic burdens of air pollution are even higher than those presented in this report. Even with the evidence that is available today, it is clear that the impacts of PM$_{2.5}$ air pollution call for urgent action from policy makers in LMICs to reduce air pollution and the resulting disease and deaths. Some key areas for action include the following:

- **Improve ground-level air-quality monitoring.** Properly operated and maintained ground-level monitoring networks for air quality provide data on the severity of air pollution, a fundamental input for effective air-quality management. Data for networks that monitor air quality are also useful for identifying the key sources that contribute to ambient air pollution. Such networks for air-quality monitoring must be subject to rigorous quality-assurance and quality-control regimes in order to ensure that the air-quality measurements generated are reliable for informing the design and implementation of interventions to reduce air pollution and protect public health. Thus, high-quality, routine air-quality monitoring, first and foremost, underpins programs for effective air-quality management that would also include (a) comprehensive emission inventories, (b) application of models to understand the transport and fate of air pollutants, (c) assessment of costs and of health and other benefits, and (d) public outreach and stakeholder engagement. It is pertinent to note that beyond initial investments in networks for air-quality monitoring, governments need to ensure effective long-term funding for sustained operation and maintenance of programs for air-quality monitoring.

- **Ensure public access to information on air quality.** To reinforce the impact of networks for air-quality monitoring, air-quality management efforts should include a robust system for dissemination of air-quality data to members of the public in formats that are widely understood and easily accessible. Public dissemination of air-quality data allows members of the public to take adequate measures to reduce their exposure to air pollution and thus provides an important social safety net for the public—particularly for vulnerable groups such as young children, the elderly, and people with health conditions that can be exacerbated by poor air quality. Public dissemination of air-quality information is also key to empower constituencies, strengthen environmental accountability, and empower stakeholders to participate in the development of interventions to improve air quality.

- **Harness innovation to drive air-quality improvements.** Technological developments can support more-targeted interventions for air-quality management while providing new avenues to engage local communities in their implementation. For instance, the Environmental Defense Fund and partners such as Google are piloting the use of low-cost sensing technologies and data analytics to provide air-quality data with a significantly higher frequency (every minute or few minutes) and resolution (for example, city block by city block). These hyperlocal monitoring networks can identify areas of poor air quality that a sparse network of traditional monitors often misses, help to better estimate actual exposure to air pollution, and even provide real-time data to help vulnerable populations make decisions that will protect their health.

- **Establish solid technical units with a clear mandate for air-quality management.** Technical units, staffed with specialists who can carry out a range of actions, including monitoring, enforcement, and planning, are indispensable to improve air quality. Such units should have clear responsibilities for designing air-quality interventions that can be endorsed by decision-makers and other stakeholders, as well as for conducting regular evaluations to assess the efficiency and effectiveness of supported interventions, identify opportunities for improvement, and incorporate new scientific evidence or emerging technologies that can drive air-quality improvements. Providing technical units with the mandate to work across sectors is paramount given that air pollution originates from a wide range of sectors, including energy, transportation, industry, and agriculture, among others.

- **Adopt regional approaches to address air pollution across boundaries.** Air pollution typically cuts across boundaries of individual cities or countries. As a result, regional airshed approaches to addressing PM$_{2.5}$ air pollution may be called for, which require federal and international collaboration of governments across multiple administrative jurisdictions and geographical boundaries to ensure effective air-quality management.

- **Prioritize key sources of PM$_{2.5}$ air pollution, notably fossil-fuel combustion, such as sulfur-emitting coal-fired power plants and diesel-fueled traffic.** Efforts to control air pollution that prioritize fossil-fuel combustion sources are most likely to return greater health benefits than broad efforts that do not consider the source and composition of PM$_{2.5}$. Sulfate—a chemical constituent of PM$_{2.5}$ from coal burning—is one of the greatest contributors to PM$_{2.5}$ toxicity and has one of the strongest associations with cardiovascular disease among the chemical constituents of PM$_{2.5}$ from fossil-fuel combustion. Reductions in PM$_{2.5}$ emissions from fossil-fuel combustion, such as sulfur-emitting coal-fired power plants and diesel vehicles, can be expected to produce the most-significant health benefits per unit of PM$_{2.5}$ reduced. Given that these sources are also key contributors to climate warming, air-pollution efforts that target these sources will also provide benefits to mitigating climate change. Notably, reducing PM$_{2.5}$ also means reducing black carbon, a component of PM$_{2.5}$ and short-lived climate pollutant.

- **Engage a wide range of instruments that are suited to reduce air pollution effectively and efficiently and ensure that they are enforced.** In order to reduce air pollution, governments need to apply the instruments and approaches that are most effective for reducing air pollution. *Command-and-control instruments* (such as standards for ambient-air quality and emission standards for vehicles and stationary sources, and vehicle inspection and maintenance programs) are well established and applied in many countries. Additional command-and-control instruments include regulations to improve fuel quality by, for example, decreasing the sulfur content of fuels. *Economic instruments* (such as air-pollution charges and repurposing of fossil-fuel subsidies) reduce air and climate pollutants while also augmenting the amount of government revenues that can be allocated to education, health care, renewable energy, and interventions to control air pollution. In addition, policies to promote conversion of vehicles from diesel to gas or to discourage the use of nitrogen-based fertilizers (which release ammonia—a precursor of secondary PM$_{2.5}$ formation) may also be used to reduce air pollution. It is important to note that effective application of the various instruments for air-quality management requires that governments put in place adequate enforcement mechanisms that also include incentives to reduce polluting behaviors.

- **Promote the use of clean cooking fuels to combat the health effects of household air pollution from solid fuels.** The populations in low- and middle-income countries using traditional cookstoves with solid fuels for cooking and other domestic purposes are exposed to PM$_{2.5}$ concentrations that are several times higher than ambient PM$_{2.5}$. Improved cookstoves, often 40 to 60 percent more energy efficient than traditional stoves, have been found to reduce exposure by around 50 percent. This reduction, however, reduces health effects by as little as 11 to 12 percent, based on analysis of the exposure-response functions from the GBD 2019. Effectively combating the health effects requires clean cooking fuels and technologies, such as LPG or electricity. Some low- and middle-income countries have already achieved a high prevalence rate of the population using clean fuels and technologies, demonstrating this possibility even at moderate GDP per capita levels.

REFERENCES

Chen, J., and G. Hoek. 2020, "Long-Term Exposure to PM and All-Cause and Cause-Specific Mortality: A Systematic Review and Meta-Analysis." *Environment International* 143. https://doi.org/10.1016/j.envint.2020.105974.

GBD 2013 Risk Factors Collaborators. 2015. "Global, Regional, and National Comparative Risk Assessment of 79 Behavioural, Environmental and Occupational, and Metabolic Risks or Clusters of Risks in 188 Countries, 1990–2013: A Systematic Analysis for the Global Burden of Disease Study 2013." *Lancet* 386: 2287–323.

GBD 2019 Risk Factors Collaborators. 2020. "Global Burden of 87 Risk Factors in 204 Countries and Territories, 1990–2019: A Systematic Analysis for the Global Burden of Disease Study 2019." *Lancet* 396: 1223–49.

Orellano, P., J. Reynoso, and N. Quaranta. 2021. "Short-Term Exposure to Sulphur Dioxide (SO_2) and All-Cause and Respiratory Mortality: A Systematic Review and Meta-Analysis." *Environment International* 150. https://doi.org/10.1016/j.envint.2021.106434.

Orellano, P., J. Reynoso, N. Quaranta, A. Bardach, and A. Ciapponi. 2020. "Short-Term Exposure to Particulate Matter (PM_{10} and $PM_{2.5}$), Nitrogen Dioxide (NO_2), and Ozone (O_3) and All-Cause and Cause-Specific Mortality: Systematic Review and Meta-Analysis." *Environment International* 142. https://doi.org/10.1016/j.envint.2020.105876.

World Bank and IHME (Institute for Health Metrics and Evaluation). 2016. *The Cost of Air Pollution: Strengthening the Economic Case for Action.* Washington, DC: World Bank.

APPENDIX A

Annual Health Damages and Costs of PM$_{2.5}$ Exposure, 2019

TABLE A.1 **Annual health damages from PM$_{2.5}$ exposure, 2019**

ECONOMY	AMBIENT PM$_{2.5}$ ($\mu G/m^3$)	SOLID-FUEL USE (POPULATION)	DEATHS FROM PM$_{2.5}$		YLDS FROM PM$_{2.5}$	
			AAP	HAP	AAP	HAP
Afghanistan	52.4	62	8,679	28,168	15,748	61,111
Albania	18.6	29	1,532	724	3,609	1,987
Algeria	32.8	0	21,613	66	89,757	412
American Samoa	6.3	18	8	6	48	45
Andorra	9.1	0	11	0	57	0
Angola	28.4	36	5,563	8,726	13,379	22,060
Antigua and Barbuda	17.6	1	30	0	161	3
Argentina	13.5	3	12,590	708	38,711	2,912
Armenia	33.7	3	3,091	78	7,849	321
Aruba	—	—	—	—	—	—
Australia	6.7	0	1,781	13	9,308	125
Austria	12.2	0	2,389	9	10,389	60
Azerbaijan	25.5	7	7,860	666	17,590	2,049
Bahamas, The	15.6	2	99	2	532	15
Bahrain	59.2	1	624	2	5,447	22
Bangladesh	63.4	76	73,976	94,789	203,529	388,497
Barbados	21.3	0	175	0	779	1
Belarus	16.4	1	8,403	96	13,940	232
Belgium	12.7	0	3,491	6	15,824	40
Belize	21.2	13	93	30	370	138
Benin	46.9	92	2,304	9,891	3,794	18,322
Bermuda	7.1	5	8	1	39	6
Bhutan	40.3	37	270	352	837	1,186
Bolivia	26.8	21	3,885	2,276	8,808	7,019
Bosnia and Herzegovina	29.5	38	3,622	1,148	12,151	4,272

(continued)

TABLE A.1, *continued*

ECONOMY	AMBIENT PM₂.₅ (μG/M³)	SOLID-FUEL USE (POPULATION)	DEATHS FROM PM₂.₅		YLDS FROM PM₂.₅	
			AAP	HAP	AAP	HAP
Botswana	24.7	39	942	636	2,355	1,925
Brazil	11.7	9	43,575	14,016	167,643	65,241
British Virgin Islands	—	—	—	—	—	—
Brunei Darussalam	7.7	1	39	1	285	6
Bulgaria	19.4	20	9,072	1,812	20,028	4,493
Burkina Faso	53.7	94	3,384	24,303	4,186	35,106
Burundi	33.3	99	977	10,004	1,674	17,415
Cabo Verde	51.1	19	319	99	892	366
Cambodia	22.1	79	3,499	14,034	8,731	46,805
Cameroon	64.5	73	10,250	12,068	20,235	26,946
Canada	7.1	0	3,765	8	16,567	63
Cayman Islands	—	—	—	—	—	—
Central African Republic	46.4	100	931	6,961	1,284	9,730
Chad	59.3	96	2,614	19,066	2,966	23,939
Channel Islands	—	—	—	—	—	—
Chile	22.8	6	5,808	330	29,554	2,570
China	47.7	36	1,423,633	363,029	4,588,122	1,496,251
Colombia	22.0	9	13,033	2,454	71,733	17,650
Comoros	17.2	79	93	552	197	1,344
Congo, Dem. Rep.	35.9	93	11,060	58,038	23,430	122,993
Congo, Rep.	39.3	60	1,803	1,638	4,886	4,803
Costa Rica	17.4	6	938	104	6,710	1,042
Côte d'Ivoire	55.6	82	6,732	16,262	12,355	33,903
Croatia	18.5	6	3,072	169	11,479	775
Cuba	17.7	2	5,845	200	24,912	1,140
Curacao	—	—	—	—	—	—
Cyprus	15.6	0	413	1	1,909	5
Czech Republic	16.8	2	6,255	80	33,999	537
Denmark	9.8	0	1,298	2	4,701	13
Djibouti	43.2	16	453	201	1,132	572
Dominica	18.6	9	33	4	155	23
Dominican Republic	17.7	8	3,798	939	8,591	2,535
Ecuador	20.0	6	4,236	476	17,433	2,792
Egypt, Arab Rep.	67.9	0	90,559	73	240,586	315
El Salvador	22.3	12	1,901	618	7,836	3,146
Equatorial Guinea	45.3	25	397	84	1,243	395
Eritrea	44.1	68	1,380	3,936	2,575	8,194
Estonia	5.9	10	160	40	523	217
Eswatini	23.3	56	344	482	794	1,338
Ethiopia	33.8	96	8,957	67,827	16,037	160,370

(continued)

TABLE A.1, *continued*

ECONOMY	AMBIENT PM₂.₅ (µG/M³)	SOLID-FUEL USE (POPULATION)	DEATHS FROM PM₂.₅ AAP	DEATHS FROM PM₂.₅ HAP	YLDS FROM PM₂.₅ AAP	YLDS FROM PM₂.₅ HAP
Faroe Islands	—	—	—	—	—	—
Fiji	11.0	28	330	302	1,117	1,307
Finland	5.6	0	385	2	1,881	22
France	11.4	0	13,245	37	43,214	218
French Polynesia	—	—	—	—	—	—
Gabon	36.7	8	821	69	2,554	253
Gambia, The	58.1	95	487	1,493	945	3,638
Georgia	17.9	34	3,112	1,594	7,222	5,132
Germany	11.8	0	27,041	30	135,725	238
Ghana	54.0	70	12,544	11,065	29,588	32,419
Gibraltar	—	—	—	—	—	—
Greece	14.3	1	5,715	41	18,472	182
Greenland	6.5	2	6	0	20	1
Grenada	21.5	3	51	2	226	12
Guam	8.2	8	31	5	144	41
Guatemala	27.6	47	3,734	5,296	12,255	20,434
Guinea	52.5	98	2,455	13,752	3,397	22,145
Guinea-Bissau	54.1	98	355	1,639	603	3,072
Guyana	20.1	5	411	55	1,311	195
Haiti	19.0	90	1,822	12,151	3,489	24,779
Honduras	22.9	49	1,783	3,875	5,130	12,149
Hong Kong SAR, China	—	—	—	—	—	—
Hungary	16.5	19	6,940	1,347	24,748	6,089
Iceland	5.7	0	16	0	84	1
India	83.2	61	979,682	606,890	2,965,720	2,524,841
Indonesia	19.4	34	106,710	76,867	342,829	448,090
Iran, Islamic Rep.	38.0	0	41,742	97	188,106	590
Iraq	48.5	0	25,378	64	82,065	325
Ireland	7.9	0	535	2	2,420	15
Isle of Man	—	—	—	—	—	—
Israel	19.8	0	2,280	4	11,164	27
Italy	16.1	0	24,666	121	110,372	1,027
Jamaica	15.3	10	938	199	4,021	986
Japan	13.5	0	39,692	95	210,849	828
Jordan	30.6	0	3,074	2	18,079	11
Kazakhstan	20.3	11	10,133	1,424	29,228	5,752
Kenya	21.6	87	5,490	22,109	14,691	67,103
Kiribati	9.5	58	18	133	41	330
Korea, Dem. People's Rep.	44.3	86	21,590	31,515	55,398	87,506

(continued)

TABLE A.1, *continued*

ECONOMY	AMBIENT PM$_{2.5}$ (μG/M³)	SOLID-FUEL USE (POPULATION)	DEATHS FROM PM$_{2.5}$		YLDS FROM PM$_{2.5}$	
			AAP	HAP	AAP	HAP
Korea, Rep.	27.4	0	21,837	15	134,392	146
Kosovo	—	—	—	—	—	—
Kuwait	61.0	0	1,526	1	11,595	11
Kyrgyz Republic	24.1	24	2,586	1,432	5,319	3,700
Lao PDR	20.5	93	1,376	6,332	3,636	17,952
Latvia	12.0	8	1,119	104	2,551	382
Lebanon	29.0	0	3,303	10	13,945	74
Lesotho	27.5	55	839	1,633	1,544	3,535
Liberia	50.6	95	656	2,714	1,600	7,451
Libya	38.6	0	3,368	8	18,094	79
Liechtenstein	—	—	—	—	—	—
Lithuania	10.4	4	1,264	61	2,740	244
Luxembourg	10.1	0	91	0	624	2
Macao SAR, China	—	—	—	—	—	—
Madagascar	17.9	98	2,246	21,459	4,679	46,535
Malawi	22.3	97	1,312	12,379	2,646	27,491
Malaysia	16.6	1	10,551	111	45,661	939
Maldives	10.9	9	49	23	294	156
Mali	60.6	99	3,246	22,580	5,044	41,679
Malta	13.0	0	147	0	682	3
Marshall Islands	9.0	26	12	24	45	98
Mauritania	66.8	52	1,411	1,208	3,181	3,501
Mauritius	14.9	1	606	14	3,343	115
Mexico	20.1	13	36,582	9,854	204,771	62,613
Micronesia, Fed. Sts.	10.4	28	32	48	78	139
Moldova	13.7	6	2,102	282	4,874	987
Monaco	11.7		15	0	51	0
Mongolia	38.1	44	2,245	1,009	3,382	1,932
Montenegro	21.3	39	564	168	1,512	520
Morocco	35.1	3	27,063	1,679	81,819	6,385
Mozambique	20.8	96	1,879	25,017	3,258	48,131
Myanmar	29.4	80	24,169	49,223	62,350	178,202
Namibia	24.2	50	789	775	1,837	2,277
Nauru	—	—	—	—	—	—
Nepal	83.1	67	17,948	21,603	44,230	64,762
Netherlands	12.0	0	4,569	6	20,543	36
New Caledonia	—	—	—	—	—	—
New Zealand	6.0	0	303	3	1,238	20
Nicaragua	20.4	44	1,002	1,735	3,829	7,711

(continued)

TABLE A.1, *continued*

ECONOMY	AMBIENT PM$_{2.5}$	SOLID-FUEL USE	DEATHS FROM PM$_{2.5}$		YLDS FROM PM$_{2.5}$	
	(μG/M³)	(POPULATION)	AAP	HAP	AAP	HAP
Niger	80.1	99	2,971	26,507	3,292	32,931
Nigeria	70.4	77	68,533	128,259	106,948	203,795
North Macedonia	30.3	27	2,751	535	7,476	1,626
Northern Mariana Islands	—	20	10	5	49	34
Norway	6.6	0	393	1	2,350	13
Oman	44.6	1	1,553	6	6,742	69
Pakistan	62.6	53	114,008	116,090	256,359	356,704
Palau	—	—	5	0	18	0
Panama	13.2	10	650	154	4,178	1,535
Papua New Guinea	16.2	85	1,181	11,169	2,919	31,702
Paraguay	12.5	33	1,045	1,193	3,426	5,103
Peru	30.8	19	8,905	2,439	30,643	16,308
Philippines	18.8	48	32,019	42,675	97,367	161,885
Poland	22.6	14	27,762	2,808	106,179	13,451
Portugal	8.3	1	2,086	34	9,794	210
Puerto Rico (US)	6.9	0	427	1	3,188	8
Qatar	76	—	539	0	7,822	1
Romania	15.7	13	14,577	2,434	36,650	7,437
Russian Federation	11.6	2	73,859	2,448	146,425	6,865
Rwanda	36.2	99	1,758	7,468	3,840	16,920
Samoa	11.0	61	41	139	122	489
San Marino	—	—	6	0	29	0
São Tomé and Príncipe	31.1	55	52	87	159	313
Saudi Arabia	61.5	1	17,795	37	87,210	485
Senegal	60.2	78	3,369	9,075	8,124	24,176
Serbia	25.4	24	10,609	1,969	30,589	6,472
Seychelles	15.6	1	35	0	220	3
Sierra Leone	51.1	97	1,542	7,813	2,327	12,562
Singapore	18.8	0	1,331	2	9,629	24
Sint Maarten (Dutch part)	—	—	—	—	—	—
Slovak Republic	18.4	1	3,472	34	11,557	148
Slovenia	17.0	10	823	62	4,151	430
Solomon Islands	12.9	90	109	1,211	144	1,815
Somalia	30.4	98	770	27,553	906	35,021
South Africa	28.7	13	24,780	4,590	92,417	21,061
South Sudan	37.6	99	1,390	7,678	2,261	15,647
Spain	9.7	1	8,880	178	49,400	1,748
Sri Lanka	20.0	61	7,261	6,643	43,062	52,603

(continued)

TABLE A.1, *continued*

ECONOMY	AMBIENT PM₂.₅ (µG/M³)	SOLID-FUEL USE (POPULATION)	DEATHS FROM PM₂.₅		YLDS FROM PM₂.₅	
			AAP	HAP	AAP	HAP
St. Kitts and Nevis	—	—	11	1	54	5
St. Lucia	21.2	3	80	5	486	32
St. Martin (French part)	—	—	—	—	—	—
St. Vincent and the Grenadines	21.1	3	62	4	268	22
Sudan	54.7	41	16,634	11,310	42,558	34,771
Suriname	21.2	9	261	47	1,191	260
Sweden	5.6	0	649	3	3,157	26
Switzerland	9.9	0	1,374	1.4	7,196	14
Syrian Arab Republic	31.0	0	10,474	18	30,779	75
Tajikistan	38.3	29	4,758	2,607	8,634	5,687
Tanzania	24.7	98	6,246	39,165	10,717	77,721
Thailand	27.4	21	32,211	7,449	171,033	64,960
Timor-Leste	15.7	81	210	1,027	525	2,996
Togo	46.2	91	1,619	5,060	3,221	11,882
Tonga	10.6	36	20	31	74	130
Trinidad and Tobago	22.0	0	890	1	4,219	8
Tunisia	30.4	0	7,337	21	31,432	140
Turkey	26.0	1	41,524	236	178,545	1,612
Turkmenistan	26.2	0	3,577	5	7,447	20
Turks and Caicos Islands	—	—	—	—	—	—
Tuvalu	—	—	2	2	6	6
Uganda	35.2	98	4,586	23,001	9,018	47,575
Ukraine	14.5	4	42,916	2,728	62,746	5,657
United Arab Emirates	43.7	—	3,252	0	25,073	2
United Kingdom	10.1	0	14,449	12	74,545	85
United States	7.7	0	47,787	150	291,895	1,237
Uruguay	9.5	2	733	53	2,083	180
Uzbekistan	34.8³	10	26,749	3,164	46,908	7,100
Vanuatu	12.9	88	54	361	118	887
Venezuela, RB	21.7	0	12,384	88	47,739	423
Vietnam	20.4	41	37,457	33,247	120,815	139,201
Virgin Islands (US)	9.0	2	31	1	126	5
West Bank and Gaza	31.3	1	1,792	28	6,663	149
Yemen, Rep.	44.5	24	11,282	9,709	22,975	22,967
Zambia	25.9	80	2,949	8,822	5,308	18,259
Zimbabwe	20.8	69	2,607	10,019	5,276	23,341

Sources: Ambient PM₂.₅ and solid-fuel use are from Health Effects Institute (HEI), *State of Global Air 2020* (Boston: HEI, 2020). www.stateofglobalair.org
Annual deaths and YLDs from PM₂.₅ are from GBD 2019 Risk Factors Collaborators, "Global Burden of 87 Risk Factors in 204 Countries and Territories, 1990–2019: A Systematic Analysis for the Global Burden of Disease Study 2019," *Lancet* 396 (2020): 1223–49.
Note: HAP = household air pollution; AAP = ambient air pollution; YLD = years lived with disability; — = not available.

TABLE A.2 **Total annual health damages from PM$_{2.5}$ exposure, 2019**

ECONOMY	DEATHS FROM PM$_{2.5}$ (AAP+HAP)	YLDS FROM PM$_{2.5}$ (AAP+HAP)	PM$_{2.5}$ DEATHS PER 100,000 POPULATION	PM$_{2.5}$ YLDS PER 100,000 POPULATION
Afghanistan	36,847	76,859	96	201
Albania	2,257	5,596	83	206
Algeria	21,680	90,169	52	215
American Samoa	14	93	24	168
Andorra	11	57	13	69
Angola	14,288	35,440	47	118
Antigua and Barbuda	30	164	34	186
Argentina	13,298	41,623	29	92
Armenia	3,169	8,170	105	271
Aruba	—	—	—	—
Australia	1,795	9,433	7	38
Austria	2,398	10,449	27	117
Azerbaijan	8,526	19,639	83	191
Bahamas, The	101	547	27	145
Bahrain	625	5,469	43	379
Bangladesh	168,765	592,027	106	372
Barbados	175	780	59	262
Belarus	8,499	14,172	89	149
Belgium	3,497	15,864	31	139
Belize	123	508	30	124
Benin	12,195	22,116	96	175
Bermuda	9	46	14	71
Bhutan	621	2,023	82	268
Bolivia	6,161	15,827	51	132
Bosnia and Herzegovina	4,770	16,423	145	498
Botswana	1,578	4,280	67	183
Brazil	57,591	232,883	27	107
British Virgin Islands	—	—	—	—
Brunei Darussalam	39	291	9	67
Bulgaria	10,884	24,521	157	354
Burkina Faso	27,687	39,291	122	173
Burundi	10,980	19,090	92	160
Cabo Verde	417	1,258	74	223
Cambodia	17,533	55,536	106	334
Cameroon	22,318	47,181	77	162
Canada	3,774	16,630	10	46
Cayman Islands	—	—	—	—
Central African Republic	7,892	11,014	149	208
Chad	21,680	26,904	132	164

(continued)

TABLE A.2, *continued*

ECONOMY	DEATHS FROM PM$_{2.5}$ AAP+HAP	YLDS FROM PM$_{2.5}$ AAP+HAP	PM$_{2.5}$ DEATHS PER 100,000 POPULATION	PM$_{2.5}$ YLDS PER 100,000 POPULATION
Channel Islands	—	—	—	—
Chile	6,139	32,124	34	177
China	1,786,662	6,084,373	126	428
Colombia	15,487	89,383	32	187
Comoros	645	1,541	90	216
Congo, Dem. Rep.	69,098	146,423	79	167
Congo, Rep.	3,441	9,688	65	184
Costa Rica	1,041	7,753	22	164
Côte d'Ivoire	22,994	46,259	88	177
Croatia	3,241	12,254	76	288
Cuba	6,045	26,052	53	229
Curacao	—	—	—	—
Cyprus	414	1,914	32	146
Czech Republic	6,335	34,535	60	324
Denmark	1,300	4,714	22	81
Djibouti	654	1,704	54	142
Dominica	37	178	54	260
Dominican Republic	4,737	11,126	44	102
Ecuador	4,712	20,225	27	115
Egypt, Arab Rep.	90,632	240,901	91	243
El Salvador	2,520	10,981	40	176
Equatorial Guinea	481	1,638	34	115
Eritrea	5,316	10,769	79	160
Estonia	200	740	15	56
Eswatini	825	2,132	72	187
Ethiopia	76,783	176,406	71	164
Faroe Islands	—	—	—	—
Fiji	633	2,423	69	266
Finland	387	1,902	7	34
France	13,282	43,431	20	66
French Polynesia	—	0	0	—
Gabon	890	2,807	51	160
Gambia, The	1,980	4,584	88	204
Georgia	4,706	12,355	128	337
Germany	27,070	135,963	32	160
Ghana	23,608	62,008	75	197
Gibraltar	—	—	—	—
Greece	5,757	18,655	56	180
Greenland	6	22	11	39

(continued)

TABLE A.2, *continued*

ECONOMY	DEATHS FROM PM$_{2.5}$ AAP+HAP	YLDS FROM PM$_{2.5}$ AAP+HAP	PM$_{2.5}$ DEATHS PER 100,000 POPULATION	PM$_{2.5}$ YLDS PER 100,000 POPULATION
Grenada	54	238	52	230
Guam	36	185	21	109
Guatemala	9,030	32,689	51	184
Guinea	16,207	25,541	128	202
Guinea-Bissau	1,994	3,675	105	193
Guyana	466	1,506	60	195
Haiti	13,973	28,267	113	228
Honduras	5,658	17,279	58	176
Hong Kong SAR, China	—	—	—	—
Hungary	8,287	30,837	86	319
Iceland	16	85	5	25
India	1,586,571	5,490,561	114	395
Indonesia	183,577	790,919	71	305
Iran, Islamic Rep.	41,839	188,696	50	224
Iraq	25,442	82,390	60	196
Ireland	537	2,435	11	50
Isle of Man	—	—	—	—
Israel	2,284	11,191	25	120
Italy	24,787	111,400	41	185
Jamaica	1,137	5,007	40	178
Japan	39,787	211,677	31	166
Jordan	3,075	18,090	26	155
Kazakhstan	11,557	34,980	63	190
Kenya	27,600	81,794	55	163
Kiribati	151	371	127	313
Korea, Dem. People's Rep.	53,105	142,904	202	545
Korea, Rep.	21,852	134,538	41	252
Kosovo	—	—	—	—
Kuwait	1,527	11,606	34	262
Kyrgyz Republic	4,018	9,020	61	138
Lao PDR	7,708	21,589	108	302
Latvia	1,223	2,933	64	153
Lebanon	3,312	14,018	64	271
Lesotho	2,472	5,079	118	243
Liberia	3,370	9,051	70	189
Libya	3,375	18,173	50	270
Liechtenstein	—	—	—	—
Lithuania	1,325	2,984	47	107
Luxembourg	91	626	15	101

(continued)

TABLE A.2, *continued*

ECONOMY	DEATHS FROM PM$_{2.5}$ AAP+HAP	YLDS FROM PM$_{2.5}$ AAP+HAP	PM$_{2.5}$ DEATHS PER 100,000 POPULATION	PM$_{2.5}$ YLDS PER 100,000 POPULATION
Macao SAR, China	—	—	—	—
Madagascar	23,706	51,214	89	192
Malawi	13,691	30,138	74	163
Malaysia	10,662	46,600	34	149
Maldives	72	450	14	90
Mali	25,827	46,723	118	213
Malta	148	684	34	156
Marshall Islands	36	143	63	251
Mauritania	2,619	6,682	65	166
Mauritius	621	3,458	49	271
Mexico	46,436	267,384	37	214
Micronesia, Fed. Sts.	80	217	79	212
Moldova	2,385	5,861	65	159
Monaco	15	51	40	135
Mongolia	3,254	5,314	96	157
Montenegro	732	2,032	118	328
Morocco	28,743	88,204	80	245
Mozambique	26,895	51,388	91	174
Myanmar	73,393	240,552	134	440
Namibia	1,564	4,114	65	171
Nauru	—	—	—	—
Nepal	39,552	108,992	130	358
Netherlands	4,575	20,579	27	120
New Caledonia	—	—	—	—
New Zealand	305	1,258	7	28
Nicaragua	2,738	11,540	42	177
Niger	29,477	36,222	127	155
Nigeria	196,793	310,743	92	145
North Macedonia	3,286	9,103	153	423
Northern Mariana Islands	16	83	36	195
Norway	394	2,363	7	44
Oman	1,559	6,811	34	149
Pakistan	230,098	613,063	103	274
Palau	5	18	25	100
Panama	804	5,713	19	137
Papua New Guinea	12,350	34,621	125	351
Paraguay	2,239	8,528	32	123
Peru	11,345	46,951	33	138
Philippines	74,693	259,252	67	231

(continued)

TABLE A.2, *continued*

ECONOMY	DEATHS FROM PM$_{2.5}$ AAP+HAP	YLDS FROM PM$_{2.5}$ AAP+HAP	PM$_{2.5}$ DEATHS PER 100,000 POPULATION	PM$_{2.5}$ YLDS PER 100,000 POPULATION
Poland	30,570	119,630	80	311
Portugal	2,120	10,005	20	94
Puerto Rico (US)	427	3,196	12	91
Qatar	539	7,823	19	273
Romania	17,010	44,087	88	229
Russian Federation	76,307	153,290	52	104
Rwanda	9,226	20,760	73	164
Samoa	180	611	85	289
San Marino	6	29	17	88
São Tomé and Príncipe	139	472	68	230
Saudi Arabia	17,832	87,695	50	245
Senegal	12,444	32,300	82	213
Serbia	12,578	37,061	144	424
Seychelles	35	224	35	219
Sierra Leone	9,355	14,890	113	180
Singapore	1,333	9,653	24	170
Sint Maarten (Dutch part)	—	—	—	—
Slovak Republic	3,506	11,705	64	215
Slovenia	885	4,581	43	221
Solomon Islands	1,320	1,958	201	299
Somalia	28,323	35,927	139	177
South Africa	29,370	113,478	53	204
South Sudan	9,068	17,909	98	193
Spain	9,058	51,149	20	111
Sri Lanka	13,904	95,665	64	438
St. Kitts and Nevis	12	59	20	99
St. Lucia	85	518	49	297
St. Martin (French part)	—	—	—	—
St. Vincent and the Grenadines	67	290	59	256
Sudan	27,944	77,330	68	189
Suriname	307	1,451	53	252
Sweden	651	3,183	6	31
Switzerland	1,375	7,210	16	82
Syrian Arab Republic	10,491	30,854	72	213
Tajikistan	7,365	14,321	78	151
Tanzania	45,412	88,438	80	156
Thailand	39,660	235,993	57	337
Timor-Leste	1,238	3,521	93	264
Togo	6,679	15,103	84	191

(continued)

TABLE A.2, *continued*

ECONOMY	DEATHS FROM PM$_{2.5}$ AAP+HAP	YLDS FROM PM$_{2.5}$ AAP+HAP	PM$_{2.5}$ DEATHS PER 100,000 POPULATION	PM$_{2.5}$ YLDS PER 100,000 POPULATION
Tonga	51	203	50	199
Trinidad and Tobago	891	4,227	64	305
Tunisia	7,358	31,572	64	273
Turkey	41,760	180,156	51	221
Turkmenistan	3,582	7,467	70	147
Turks and Caicos Islands	—	—	—	—
Tuvalu	4	12	32	104
Uganda	27,587	56,593	67	138
Ukraine	45,643	68,403	104	155
United Arab Emirates	3,252	25,075	35	271
United Kingdom	14,461	74,630	22	111
United States	47,937	293,133	15	89
Uruguay	786	2,263	23	66
Uzbekistan	29,913	54,008	89	160
Vanuatu	416	1,006	141	341
Venezuela, RB	12,471	48,162	44	172
Vietnam	70,703	260,016	73	270
Virgin Islands (US)	32	131	31	126
West Bank and Gaza	1,820	6,811	37	137
Yemen, Rep.	20,991	45,942	67	146
Zambia	11,771	23,567	65	129
Zimbabwe	12,626	28,618	84	191

Source: GBD 2019 Risk Factors Collaborators, "Global Burden of 87 Risk Factors in 204 Countries and Territories, 1990–2019: A Systematic Analysis for the Global Burden of Disease Study 2019," *Lancet* 396 (2020): 1223–49.
Note: HAP = household air pollution; AAP = ambient air pollution; YLDs = years lived with disability; — = not available.

TABLE A.3 **Annual cost of health damages from PM$_{2.5}$ exposure, 2019**

ECONOMY	US$, MILLIONS AAP	HAP	TOTAL	$ (PPP), MILLIONS AAP	HAP	TOTAL	% OF GDP EQUIVALENT	MORBIDITY COST SHARE (%)
Afghanistan	312	1,047	1,359	1,425	4,781	6,206	7.1	19
Albania	784	377	1,160	2,122	1,020	3,142	7.6	11
Algeria	9,385	32	9,417	28,095	97	28,192	5.5	25
American Samoa	—	—	—	—	—	—	—	—
Andorra	—	—	—	—	—	—	—	—
Angola	1,407	2,222	3,630	3,280	5,179	8,458	3.8	13
Antigua and Barbuda	72	1	73	92	2	94	4.2	15
Argentina	13,176	766	13,942	30,217	1,757	31,974	3.1	10
Armenia	1,412	39	1,450	4,342	119	4,462	10.6	14

(continued)

TABLE A.3, *continued*

ECONOMY	US$, MILLIONS			$ (PPP), MILLIONS			% OF GDP EQUIVALENT	MORBIDITY COST SHARE (%)
	AAP	HAP	TOTAL	AAP	HAP	TOTAL		
Aruba	—	—	—	—	—	—	—	—
Australia	11,418	97	11,516	11,088	95	11,183	0.8	18
Austria	13,481	54	13,535	15,850	64	15,913	3.0	16
Azerbaijan	3,394	292	3,686	10,621	914	11,535	7.7	4
Bahamas, The	383	8	391	433	10	442	3.0	12
Bahrain	1,671	5	1,676	3,334	10	3,344	4.3	13
Bangladesh	11,173	15,365	26,538	29,808	40,989	70,798	8.8	18
Barbados	459	1	460	412	0	413	8.8	16
Belarus	5,480	64	5,544	16,401	193	16,593	8.8	7
Belgium	19,198	35	19,233	22,706	41	22,748	3.6	20
Belize	41	13	54	62	20	82	2.9	19
Benin	206	898	1,105	579	2,522	3,101	7.7	13
Bermuda	—	—	—	—	—	—	—	—
Bhutan	94	125	219	333	441	774	8.5	20
Bolivia	1,184	716	1,901	3,030	1,832	4,862	4.6	10
Bosnia and Herzegovina	2,377	769	3,147	6,181	2,001	8,182	15.7	20
Botswana	716	490	1,206	1,665	1,138	2,803	6.6	6
Brazil	38,830	12,888	51,719	67,970	22,560	90,530	2.8	16
British Virgin Islands	—	—	—	—	—	—	—	—
Brunei Darussalam	137	3	140	285	5	291	1.0	19
Bulgaria	9,229	1,863	11,092	23,278	4,699	27,978	16.3	9
Burkina Faso	173	1,264	1,437	509	3,720	4,229	9.1	11
Burundi	14	148	163	43	445	488	5.4	16
Cabo Verde	100	33	133	208	67	276	6.7	15
Cambodia	440	1,829	2,268	1,223	5,086	6,310	8.4	13
Cameroon	1,135	1,356	2,491	2,883	3,444	6,327	6.4	12
Canada	20,022	48	20,070	22,253	54	22,306	1.2	16
Cayman Islands	—	—	—	—	—	—	—	—
Central African Republic	23	170	193	48	357	405	8.7	4
Chad	115	850	965	267	1,970	2,237	8.5	11
Channel Islands	—	—	—	—	—	—	—	—
Chile	11,102	674	11,776	18,747	1,138	19,885	4.2	13
China	1,465,524	386,116	1,851,640	2,397,105	631,557	3,028,662	12.9	12
Colombia	9,271	1,859	11,130	22,547	4,521	27,069	3.4	22
Comoros	10	62	73	24	144	167	6.1	21
Congo, Dem. Rep.	382	2,006	2,388	801	4,206	5,008	5.0	19
Congo, Rep.	279	257	536	477	439	916	5.0	17
Costa Rica	1,435	176	1,611	2,395	294	2,689	2.6	27

(continued)

TABLE A.3, *continued*

ECONOMY	US$, MILLIONS			$ (PPP), MILLIONS			% OF GDP EQUIVALENT	MORBIDITY COST SHARE (%)
	AAP	HAP	TOTAL	AAP	HAP	TOTAL		
Côte d'Ivoire	1,235	3,031	4,266	2,947	7,234	10,180	7.3	13
Croatia	5,883	335	6,218	11,872	677	12,549	10.3	16
Cuba	—	—	—	—	—	—	—	—
Curacao	—	—	—	—	—	—	—	—
Cyprus	1,340	3	1,342	1,984	4	1,988	4.0	13
Czech Republic	17,422	233	17,654	32,108	429	32,536	7.2	17
Denmark	8,566	15	8,581	8,567	15	8,582	2.5	15
Djibouti	131	59	191	221	100	321	5.7	17
Dominica	28	4	32	43	6	48	5.3	19
Dominican Republic	3,225	815	4,040	7,469	1,888	9,357	4.5	12
Ecuador	2,520	301	2,821	4,828	576	5,404	2.6	15
Egypt, Arab Rep.	25,958	23	25,981	105,299	92	105,391	8.6	13
El Salvador	767	260	1,028	1,674	569	2,243	3.8	20
Equatorial Guinea	331	74	405	788	176	964	3.7	12
Eritrea	—	—	—	—	—	—	—	—
Estonia	437	118	556	717	194	911	1.8	13
Eswatini	124	180	304	292	424	716	6.9	19
Ethiopia	512	4,008	4,519	1,379	10,804	12,183	4.7	13
Faroe Islands	—	—	—	—	—	—	—	—
Fiji	206	197	403	479	457	935	7.3	16
Finland	2,229	16	2,244	2,349	17	2,366	0.8	19
France	61,275	189	61,464	74,805	231	75,036	2.3	15
French Polynesia	—	—	—	—	—	—	—	—
Gabon	607	52	659	1,225	105	1,330	4.0	10
Gambia, The	26	82	108	79	252	331	6.1	18
Georgia	1,416	750	2,166	4,644	2,459	7,103	12.2	10
Germany	146,383	178	146,561	177,374	216	177,590	3.8	19
Ghana	2,254	2,050	4,304	5,769	5,248	11,017	6.4	14
Gibraltar	—	—	—	—	—	—	—	—
Greece	13,393	100	13,493	21,475	161	21,636	6.4	11
Greenland	—	—	—	—	—	—	—	—
Grenada	60	3	63	98	5	103	5.1	16
Guam	—	—	—	—	—	—	—	—
Guatemala	1,555	2,257	3,811	3,027	4,394	7,421	5.0	15
Guinea	174	990	1,165	438	2,485	2,923	8.6	9
Guinea-Bissau	16	76	93	48	226	275	6.9	13
Guyana	213	29	242	394	53	447	5.7	16
Haiti	89	597	686	212	1,425	1,637	8.1	13
Honduras	393	866	1,259	910	2,007	2,917	5.0	17

(continued)

TABLE A.3, *continued*

ECONOMY	US$, MILLIONS			$ (PPP), MILLIONS			% OF GDP EQUIVALENT	MORBIDITY COST SHARE (%)
	AAP	HAP	TOTAL	AAP	HAP	TOTAL		
Hong Kong SAR, China	—	—	—	—	—	—	—	—
Hungary	13,892	2,793	16,685	28,650	5,760	34,410	10.4	14
Iceland	123	1	124	111	1	111	0.5	21
India	184,291	121,397	305,689	616,091	405,835	1,021,926	10.6	19
Indonesia	41,396	32,602	73,998	123,137	96,979	220,116	6.6	15
Iran, Islamic Rep.	23,610	57	23,667	62,132	151	62,283	5.0	13
Iraq	14,331	39	14,369	27,270	74	27,344	6.1	14
Ireland	4,353	18	4,370	4,883	20	4,903	1.1	16
Isle of Man	—	—	—	—	—	—	—	—
Israel	12,096	22	12,117	11,694	21	11,716	3.1	17
Italy	98,553	556	99,109	131,238	741	131,978	5.0	17
Jamaica	517	113	630	941	206	1,147	3.8	19
Japan	194,886	520	195,406	209,359	558	209,917	3.8	18
Jordan	1,596	1	1,597	3,803	2	3,805	3.7	33
Kazakhstan	10,497	1,525	12,022	29,604	4,302	33,905	6.7	9
Kenya	769	3,148	3,917	1,910	7,814	9,724	4.1	13
Kiribati	2	15	17	3	22	25	8.9	13
Korea, Dem. People's Rep.	—	—	—	—	—	—	—	—
Korea, Rep.	84,385	64	84,449	114,318	87	114,405	5.1	17
Kosovo	—	—	—	—	—	—	—	—
Kuwait	5,306	2	5,309	8,599	4	8,603	3.9	11
Kyrgyz Republic	275	157	432	1,147	656	1,804	5.1	14
Lao PDR	297	1,374	1,671	954	4,419	5,373	9.2	11
Latvia	2,311	226	2,536	4,172	407	4,579	7.4	8
Lebanon	2,735	9	2,744	5,385	18	5,403	5.1	18
Lesotho	69	138	207	172	343	515	8.4	14
Liberia	26	111	138	63	266	329	4.5	17
Libya	2,827	8	2,835	5,815	16	5,831	5.4	20
Liechtenstein	—	—	—	—	—	—	—	—
Lithuania	2,702	138	2,840	5,307	271	5,578	5.2	7
Luxembourg	1,140	3	1,143	1,206	3	1,209	1.6	25
Macao SAR, China	—	—	—	—	—	—	—	—
Madagascar	75	717	792	245	2,355	2,600	5.6	12
Malawi	32	311	343	87	833	920	4.5	16
Malaysia	13,977	168	14,145	36,153	434	36,587	3.9	15
Maldives	59	28	87	107	52	159	1.5	19
Mali	196	1,396	1,592	534	3,798	4,333	9.1	13
Malta	512	1	513	794	2	797	3.5	16

(continued)

TABLE A.3, *continued*

ECONOMY	US$, MILLIONS			$ (PPP), MILLIONS			% OF GDP EQUIVALENT	MORBIDITY COST SHARE (%)
	AAP	HAP	TOTAL	AAP	HAP	TOTAL		
Marshall Islands	—	—	—	—	—	—	—	—
Mauritania	199	178	377	642	575	1,216	5.0	18
Mauritius	764	19	783	1,632	41	1,674	5.5	16
Mexico	39,513	10,875	50,388	81,769	22,504	104,273	4.0	16
Micronesia, Fed. Sts.	—	—	—	—	—	—	—	—
Moldova	940	136	1,076	2,837	410	3,246	9.0	16
Monaco	—	—	—	—	—	—	—	—
Mongolia	864	395	1,260	2,579	1,180	3,760	9.1	7
Montenegro	526	159	685	1,369	415	1,784	12.5	11
Morocco	7,995	519	8,513	19,527	1,267	20,794	7.3	18
Mozambique	55	740	795	149	2,007	2,156	5.3	11
Myanmar	2,758	5,916	8,673	10,490	22,503	32,992	11.4	16
Namibia	356	362	718	722	732	1,454	5.8	14
Nauru	—	—	—	—	—	—	—	—
Nepal	1,398	1,723	3,121	4,645	5,723	10,368	10.2	12
Netherlands	26,920	35	26,955	30,635	40	30,676	3.0	16
New Caledonia	—	—	—	—	—	—	—	—
New Zealand	1,466	14	1,479	1,531	14	1,545	0.7	13
Nicaragua	168	300	468	495	883	1,378	3.7	21
Niger	95	856	951	217	1,960	2,177	7.4	9
Nigeria	12,172	22,829	35,001	29,196	54,756	83,951	7.8	12
North Macedonia	1,689	333	2,022	4,939	973	5,912	15.9	11
Northern Mariana Islands	—	—	—	—	—	—	—	—
Norway	3,382	11	3,393	2,997	10	3,006	0.8	19
Oman	2,816	12	2,828	5,287	23	5,310	3.7	7
Pakistan	11,943	12,845	24,788	45,413	48,840	94,253	8.9	18
Palau	10	0	10	11	0	11	3.4	11
Panama	1,273	326	1,599	2,651	679	3,330	2.4	16
Papua New Guinea	281	2,727	3,008	451	4,380	4,831	12.0	20
Paraguay	552	656	1,208	1,346	1,600	2,947	3.2	15
Peru	5,661	1,657	7,317	10,855	3,177	14,032	3.2	9
Philippines	9,825	13,446	23,271	26,154	35,794	61,949	6.2	12
Poland	52,600	5,501	58,101	115,411	12,070	127,481	9.8	14
Portugal	5,954	101	6,055	9,382	159	9,541	2.5	16
Puerto Rico (US)	2,065	4	2,069	2,259	4	2,263	2.0	29
Qatar	3,461	0	3,462	5,156	0	5,156	1.9	14
Romania	21,741	3,691	25,433	54,351	9,228	63,579	10.2	8
Russian Federation	92,510	3,177	95,686	233,022	8,002	241,024	5.7	9
Rwanda	101	432	533	292	1,249	1,541	5.3	17
Samoa	17	59	76	26	93	119	8.9	24

(continued)

TABLE A.3, *continued*

ECONOMY	US$, MILLIONS			$ (PPP), MILLIONS			% OF GDP EQUIVALENT	MORBIDITY COST SHARE (%)
	AAP	HAP	TOTAL	AAP	HAP	TOTAL		
San Marino	—	—	—	—	—	—	—	—
São Tomé and Príncipe	9	17	26	20	34	54	6.1	29
Saudi Arabia	45,216	111	45,327	95,568	235	95,803	5.7	11
Senegal	381	1,046	1,427	932	2,555	3,487	6.1	18
Serbia	8,172	1,544	9,716	20,964	3,961	24,925	18.9	13
Seychelles	80	1	81	140	2	141	4.8	18
Sierra Leone	50	257	308	179	913	1,092	7.8	13
Singapore	8,976	16	8,992	13,949	25	13,974	2.4	18
Sint Maarten (Dutch part)	—	—	—	—	—	—	—	—
Slovak Republic	7,944	81	8,025	14,047	143	14,191	7.6	11
Slovenia	2,675	216	2,891	4,226	341	4,567	5.4	20
Solomon Islands	15	170	185	18	197	214	13.0	9
Somalia	—	—	—	—	—	—	—	—
South Africa	15,298	2,953	18,251	33,135	6,397	39,532	5.2	19
South Sudan								
Spain	32,814	755	33,569	46,776	1,076	47,852	2.4	19
Sri Lanka	3,380	3,401	6,781	11,947	12,023	23,971	8.1	33
St. Kitts and Nevis	28	2	30	38	3	42	2.9	15
St. Lucia	101	6	107	140	8	148	5.0	19
St. Martin (French part)	—	—	—	—	—	—	—	—
St. Vincent and the Grenadines	46	3	50	81	6	86	6.0	16
Sudan	613	434	1,047	5,726	4,050	9,776	5.5	21
Suriname	194	36	231	482	90	572	5.8	19
Sweden	3,823	19	3,842	4,135	20	4,155	0.7	17
Switzerland	12,661	15	12,676	10,962	13	10,975	1.8	19
Syrian Arab Republic	—	—	—	—	—	—	—	—
Tajikistan	307	173	480	1,242	698	1,941	5.9	14
Tanzania	473	3,007	3,480	1,168	7,424	8,592	5.3	10
Thailand	26,260	6,581	32,841	64,667	16,207	80,874	6.0	14
Timor-Leste	20	102	122	51	256	308	7.3	17
Togo	76	245	320	186	602	788	5.9	22
Tonga	8	13	21	12	19	31	4.5	21
Trinidad and Tobago	1,878	3	1,881	2,964	5	2,969	7.8	10
Tunisia	2,530	8	2,538	8,543	28	8,571	6.5	22
Turkey	43,168	267	43,435	133,074	822	133,896	5.8	15
Turkmenistan	2,408	4	2,412	5,435	9	5,443	5.8	9

(continued)

TABLE A.3, *continued*

ECONOMY	US$, MILLIONS			$ (PPP), MILLIONS			% OF GDP EQUIVALENT	MORBIDITY COST SHARE (%)
	AAP	HAP	TOTAL	AAP	HAP	TOTAL		
Turks and Caicos Islands	—	—	—	—	—	—	—	—
Tuvalu	1	1	1	1	1	1	2.6	15
Uganda	246	1,245	1,491	721	3,640	4,361	4.3	15
Ukraine	14,283	935	15,218	52,077	3,409	55,486	9.4	7
United Arab Emirates	14,748	1	14,748	23,916	1	23,917	3.5	13
United Kingdom	73,528	65	73,593	84,669	74	84,744	2.6	19
United States	371,321	1,256	372,576	371,321	1,256	372,576	1.7	22
Uruguay	1,473	107	1,580	2,042	149	2,191	2.8	8
Uzbekistan	3,782	458	4,241	15,984	1,937	17,921	7.3	9
Vanuatu	12	82	95	13	88	101	10.3	14
Venezuela, RB	—	—	—	—	—	—	—	—
Vietnam	8,869	8,149	17,017	27,352	25,132	52,485	6.5	13
Virgin Islands (US)	—	—	—	—	—	—	—	—
West Bank and Gaza	563	10	573	1,056	19	1,074	3.8	27
Yemen, Rep.	—	—	—	—	—	—	—	—
Zambia	279	849	1,128	783	2,382	3,165	4.9	12
Zimbabwe	271	1,060	1,331	547	2,138	2,685	6.2	13

Sources: Annual cost is estimated using the methodologies in appendixes B–D.

Note: HAP = household air pollution; AAP = ambient air pollution. ; — = not available Cost of health damages of PM$_{2.5}$ is not estimated for some countries and territories due to lack of estimate of deaths from PM$_{2.5}$ in the GBD 2019 study or absence of GDP per capita (PPP) in the World Development Indicators database.

Health Damages of PM$_{2.5}$

Particulate matter, and especially fine particulates (PM$_{2.5}$), is the air pollutant that globally is associated with the largest health damages. Health damages of PM$_{2.5}$ exposure include both premature mortality and morbidity. The most substantial health damages of PM$_{2.5}$ are cardiovascular disease, COPD, lung cancer, LRI, type 2 diabetes, and neonatal disorders (GBD 2019 study). The methodologics to estimate these health damages have evolved as the body of research evidence has increased.

Two decades ago, Pope et al. (2002) found elevated risk of cardiopulmonary (CP) and lung cancer mortality from long-term exposure to ambient PM$_{2.5}$ in a study of a large population of adults 30 or more years of age in the United States. CP mortality includes mortality from respiratory infections, cardiovascular disease, and chronic respiratory disease. The World Health Organization used the study by Pope et al. when estimating global mortality from outdoor air pollution (Ezzati et al. 2004; WHO 2009). A decade ago, research suggested that the *marginal increase* in relative risk of mortality from PM$_{2.5}$ declines with increasing concentrations of PM$_{2.5}$ (Pope et al. 2009, 2011). Pope et al. (2009, 2011) derive a shape of the PM$_{2.5}$ exposure-response curve based on studies of mortality from active cigarette smoking, secondhand cigarette smoking (SHS), and outdoor PM$_{2.5}$ air pollution.

AN INTEGRATED EXPOSURE-RESPONSE FUNCTION

The GBD 2010–19 studies take Pope et al. (2009, 2011) some steps further by deriving an integrated exposure-response (IER) function that relates relative risk (RR) of various disease outcomes to the level of exposure to fine particulate matter pollution (PM$_{2.5}$) both in the ambient and household environments (Burnett et al. 2014; Shin et al. 2013).

The parameter values of the IER risk function in the GBD 2019 study are derived from studies of health outcomes associated with long-term exposure to ambient particulate-matter pollution, secondhand tobacco smoking, and household air pollution from solid cooking fuels (GBD 2019 Risk Factors Collaborators 2020, Supplement). This provides a risk function that can be applied to a wide range of ambient PM$_{2.5}$ concentrations around the world as well as to high household air-pollution levels of PM$_{2.5}$ from combustion of solid fuels.

The disease outcomes assessed using the IER function are IHD, stroke, lung cancer, COPD, LRI, and type 2 diabetes. The relative risks for IHD and stroke are age-specific with five-year age intervals from 25 years of age, while singular age-group risk functions are applied for lung cancer, COPD, LRI, and type 2 diabetes. Estimation of neonatal disorders from PM$_{2.5}$ exposure follows a somewhat different approach (GBD 2019 Risk Factors Collaborators 2020, Supplement).

The method for estimating the health effects of PM$_{2.5}$ exposure is explained in GBD 2019 Risk Factors Collaborators (2020).[1] The GBD 2019 first estimates the total joint health effects of ambient PM$_{2.5}$ and household air pollution PM$_{2.5}$ from household use of solid fuels for cooking, and then apportions the health effects to ambient PM$_{2.5}$ and household air pollution PM$_{2.5}$. The total annual health effects of annual PM$_{2.5}$ exposure are estimated as follows:

$$B = D * PAF_{PM} \tag{B.1}$$

where B is annual number cases of deaths or illness from PM$_{2.5}$ among the exposed population, D is annual baseline number of cases of deaths or illness among this population, and PAF_{PM} (population-attributable fraction) is the fraction of baseline cases that is attributable to PM$_{2.5}$ exposure among this population. PAF_{PM} and B are calculated for each type of health effect covered by the GBD 2019. Annual baseline cases, D, for each type of health effect for Mexico is taken from the GBD 2019.[2]

The population-attributable fraction (PAF) for each health effect included in the GBD 2019 is calculated as follows:

$$PAF_{PM} = \frac{P_A(RR_A-1)+P_H\left(RR_H-1\right)}{P_A\left(RR_A-1\right)+P_H\left(RR_H-1\right)+1} \tag{B.2}$$

where P_A is the share of the population that is exposed only to ambient PM$_{2.5}$ (that is, the population not using solid fuels for cooking), P_H is the share of the population that uses solid fuels for cooking, RR_A is the relative risk of health effects from ambient PM$_{2.5}$ among the population exposed only to ambient PM$_{2.5}$, and RR_H is the relative risk of health effects from PM$_{2.5}$ among the population exposed to household air pollution PM$_{2.5}$. As the whole population is exposed to at least some level of ambient PM$_{2.5}$, then $P_A + P_H = 1$.

The size of the relative risks of health effects among the population only exposed to ambient PM$_{2.5}$ is:

$$RR_A = RR(AAP) / RR(TMREL) \tag{B.3}$$

where $RR(AAP)$ is the relative risk of health effects at annual PM$_{2.5}$ = AAP and $RR(TMREL)$ is the relative risk at PM$_{2.5}$ = TMREL (theoretical minimum-risk exposure level). These relative risks are reported by the GBD 2019 for each type of health effect for a range of annual PM$_{2.5}$ from 0.01 to 2,500 µg/m^3.[3] TMREL may be chosen within the range of 2.4–5.9 µg/m^3 that is used by the GBD 2019 or may be chosen to be larger or smaller. TRMEL may also be chosen as zero, in which case $RR(TMREL)$ = 1.

The size of the relative risks of health effects among the population exposed to household air pollution PM$_{2.5}$ is:

$$RR_H = RR(HAP + AAP) / RR\ (TMREL) \tag{B.4}$$

where $RR(HAP + AAP)$ is the relative risk at exposure level $PM_{2.5}$ = HAP + AAP. This exposure level includes both exposure to $PM_{2.5}$ from the use of solid fuels (HAP) and exposure to ambient $PM_{2.5}$ (AAP). HAP + AAP is a so-called personal-exposure level that is typically measured over a 24- to 48-hour period by a measurement device attached to a person (and assumed to reflect long-term exposure). The exposure level is generally different for each household member due to differences in activity patterns. Most studies measuring personal exposure have been for adult women, who usually are exposed to the highest level of $PM_{2.5}$ in households cooking with solid fuels. The GBD 2019 uses a fraction of the adult-women exposure level equal to 0.64 for adult men and 0.85 for children. Because of these differences in exposure levels, PAF is calculated separately for adult females, adult males, and children under the age of five years.

The GBD 2019 then apportions the PAF_{PM} to ambient and household air pollution as follows:

$$PAF_{AAP} = \frac{AAP}{AAP + P_H HAP} * PAF_{PM} \tag{B.5}$$

$$PAF_{HAP} = \frac{P_H HAP}{AAP + P_H HAP} * PAF_{PM} \tag{B.6}$$

where PAF_{AAP} and PAF_{HAP} are the population-attributable fractions of deaths and illnesses due to ambient $PM_{2.5}$ and household air pollution $PM_{2.5}$ from the use of solid fuels, respectively; AAP is annual ambient $PM_{2.5}$; HAP is personal $PM_{2.5}$ exposure from the use of solid fuels; and P_H is the share of the population using solid fuels for cooking.

This approach to apportioning the health effects of $PM_{2.5}$ ensures that

$$PAF_{PM} = PAF_{AAP} + PAF_{HAP} \tag{B.7}$$

The GBD 2019 estimates PAF_{PM}, PAF_{AAP} and PAF_{HAP} at small geographic units over which health effects are summed to the national, state, province, or city level. Each geographic area is a 0.1° x 0.1° grid (corresponding to 11 km x 11 km at the equator).

However, equations B.5–B.6 are less accurate if the *PAFs* are estimated for large geographic units with a single population-weighted $PM_{2.5}$ exposure level applied to each unit. In this case, an alternative approach to apportioning the health effects uses the following three steps:

Step 1:

$$PAF_{AAP}^P = \frac{P_A(RR_A - 1)}{P_A(RR_A - 1) + 1} \tag{B.8}$$

$$PAF_{HAP}^P = \frac{P_H(RR_H - 1)}{P_H(RR_H - 1) + 1} \tag{B.9}$$

which are "partial" *PAFs* for the population exposed only to ambient $PM_{2.5}$ and the population exposed to household air pollution (the population using solid fuels). RR_H in the "partial" *PAF* for household air pollution is for exposure level $HAP + AAP$. The next step involves separating the effects of AAP and HAP in equation B.9 and adding the effects to the *PAFs* in equations B.8–B.9.

Step 2:

$$PAF_{AAP}^{F} = PAF_{AAP}^{P} + PAF_{HAP}^{P} * AAP / (AAP + HAP) \tag{B.10}$$

$$PAF_{HAP}^{F} = PAF_{HAP}^{P} * HAP / (AAP + HAP) \tag{B.11}$$

The result in step 2 is such that

$$PAF_{AAP}^{F} + PAF_{HAP}^{F} > PAF_{PM} \tag{B.12}$$

The final step involves adjusting the two *PAFs* downwards so that the sum is equal to *PAF$_{PM}$*.

Step 3:

$$PAF_{AAP}^{'} = \frac{PAF_{AAP}^{F}}{PAF_{AAP}^{F} + PAF_{HAP}^{F}} * PAF_{PM} \tag{B.13}$$

$$PAF_{HAP}^{'} = \frac{PAF_{HAP}^{F}}{PAF_{AAP}^{F} + PAF_{HAP}^{F}} * PAF_{PM} \tag{B.14}$$

The two *PAFs* give identical *PAFs* for $P_H = 0$ and $P_H = 1.0$. However, for $0 < P_H < 1$, the GBD approach results in a smaller PAF for ambient PM$_{2.5}$ and a larger PAF for household air pollution PM$_{2.5}$ than the alternative approach described in steps 1–3. The difference can be quite large when PM$_{2.5}$ exposure from household air pollution is substantially higher than from ambient PM$_{2.5}$, and increases as P_H approaches 0.5 from 0 and from 1.0. Therefore, the approach in steps 1–3 is recommended if estimation of health effects of air pollution is undertaken with exposure data reflecting relatively large geographic units, such as city by city, state by state, province by province, or urban and rural.

NOTES

1. Supplementary Appendix 1 (pp. 78–115).
2. www.healthdata.org.
3. http://ghdx.healthdata.org/record/ihme-data/global-burden-disease-study-2019 -gbd-2019-particulate-matter-risk-curves.

REFERENCES

Burnett, Richard T., C. Arden Pope III, Majid Ezzati, Casey Olives, Stephen S. Lim, Sumi Mehta, Hwashin H. Shin, Gitanjali Singh, Bryan Hubbell, Michael Brauer, H. Ross Anderson, Kirk R. Smith, John R. Balmes, Nigel G. Bruce, Haidong Kan, Francine Laden, Annette Prüss-Ustün, Michelle C. Turner, Susan M. Gapstur, W. Ryan Diver, and Aaron Cohen. 2014. "An Integrated Risk Function for Estimating the Global Burden of Disease Attributable to Ambient Fine Particulate Matter Exposure." *Environmental Health Perspectives*: 122 (4): 397–403.

Ezzati, M., A. D. Lopez, A. A. Rodgers, and C. J. Murray. 2004. *Comparative Quantification of Health Risks: Global and Regional Burden of Disease Attributable to Selected Major Risk Factors*. Geneva: WHO.

GBD 2019 Risk Factors Collaborators. 2020. "Global Burden of 87 Risk Factors in 204 Countries and Territories, 1990–2019: A Systematic Analysis for the Global Burden of Disease Study 2019." *Lancet* 396: 1223–49.

Pope, C. A., III, R. T. Burnett, D. Krewski, M. Jerrett, Y. Shi, E. E. Calle, and M. J. Thun. 2009. "Cardiovascular Mortality and Exposure to Airborne Fine Particulate Matter and Cigarette Smoke: Shape of the Exposure-Response Relationship." *Circulation* 120: 941–48.

Pope, C. A., III, R. T. Burnett, M. J. Thun, E. E. Calle, D. Krewski, K. Ito, and G. Thurston. 2002. "Lung Cancer, Cardiopulmonary Mortality, and Long-Term Exposure to Fine Particulate Air Pollution." *Journal of the American Medical Association* 287: 1132–41.

Pope, C. A., III, R. T. Burnett, M. Turner, A. Cohen, D. Krewski, M. Jerrett, S. M. Gapstur, and M. J. Thun. 2011. "Lung Cancer and Cardiovascular Disease Mortality Associated with Ambient Air Pollution and Cigarette Smoke: Shape of the Exposure-Response Relationships." *Environmental Health Perspectives* 119 (11): 1616–21.

Shin, H., A. Cohen, C. A. Pope III, M. Ezzati, S. S. Lim, B. Hubbel, and R. T. Burnett. 2013. "Critical Issues in Combining Disparate Sources of Information to Estimate the Global Burden of Disease Attributable to Ambient Fine Particulate Matter Exposure." Working Paper prepared for Harvard Center for Risk Analysis "Methods for Research Synthesis: A Cross-Disciplinary Workshop," October 3.

WHO (World Health Organization). 2009. *Estimated Deaths and DALYs Attributable to Selected Environmental Risk Factors, by WHO Member States, 2004.* http://www.who.int/quantifying _ehimpacts/national/countryprofile/intro/en/index.htm.

APPENDIX C

Valuation of Premature Mortality

The predominant measure of the welfare cost of premature death used by economists is the value of statistical life (VSL). VSL is based on valuation of mortality risk. Everyone in society is constantly facing a certain risk of dying. Examples of such risks are occupational fatality risk, risk of traffic accident fatality, and environmental mortality risks. It has been observed that individuals adjust their behavior and decisions in relation to such risks. For instance, individuals demand a higher wage (a wage premium) for a job that involves a higher occupational risk of fatal accident than in other jobs, individuals may purchase safety equipment to reduce the risk of death, and/or individuals and families may be willing to pay a premium or higher rent for properties (land and buildings) in a cleaner and less polluted neighborhood or city.

Through the observation of individuals' choices and willingness to pay for reducing mortality risk (or minimum amounts that individuals require to accept a higher mortality risk), it is possible to estimate the value to society of reducing mortality risk, or, equivalently, measure the welfare cost of a particular mortality risk. For instance, it may be observed that a certain health hazard has a mortality risk of 2.5/10,000. This means that 2.5 individuals die from this hazard for every 10,000 individuals exposed. If each individual on average is willing to pay US$40 for eliminating this mortality risk, then every 10,000 individuals are collectively willing to pay US$400,000. Dividing this amount by the risk gives the VSL of US$160,000. Mathematically it can be expressed as follows:

$$VSL = WTP_{Ave} * 1/R \qquad (C.1)$$

where WTP_{Ave} is the average willingness to pay per individual for a mortality-risk reduction of magnitude R. In the illustration above, $R = 2.5/10,000$ (or $R = 0.00025$) and $WTP_{Ave} = US\$40$. Thus, if 10 individuals die from the health risk illustrated above, the cost to society is $10* VSL = 10* US\$0.16$ million $= US\$1.6$ million.

The main approaches to estimating VSL are through revealed preferences and stated preferences of people's WTP for a reduction in mortality risk or their willingness to accept (WTA) an increase in mortality risk. Most of the studies of revealed preferences are hedonic wage studies, which estimate labor market wage differentials associated with differences in occupational mortality risk. Most of the stated-preference studies rely on contingent valuation methods (CVM), which in various forms ask individuals about their WTP for mortality-risk reduction.

Studies of WTP for a reduction in risk of mortality have been carried out in numerous countries. A commonly used approach to estimate VSL in a specific country without such studies is therefore to use a benefit transfer (BT) based on meta-analyses of WTP studies from other countries. Several meta-analyses have been conducted in the last two decades. Meta-analyses assess characteristics that determine VSL, such as household income, size of risk reduction, other individual and household characteristics, and often characteristics of the methodologies used in the original WTP studies.

Most of the meta-analyses of VSL are entirely or predominantly based on hedonic wage studies. However, a meta-analysis prepared for the OECD is exclusively based on stated-preference studies, arguably of greater relevance for valuation of mortality risk from environmental factors than hedonic wage studies (Lindhjem et al. 2011; Navrud and Lindhjem 2010; OECD 2012). These stated-preference studies are from a database of more than 1,000 VSL estimates from multiple studies in over 30 countries, including in developing countries (www.oecd.org/env/policies/VSL).

Narain and Sall (2016) present a benefit-transfer methodology for valuing mortality from environmental health risks, drawing on the empirical literature of VSL, especially OECD (2012). The methodology is applied in the publication by the World Bank and IHME (2016) on the global cost of air pollution, and in the recent publication by World Bank (2020) on the global health cost of ambient air pollution. The proposed benefit-transfer function is:

$$VSL_{c,n} = VSL_{OECD} * \left(\frac{Y_{c,n}}{Y_{OECD}} \right)^{\epsilon} \tag{C.2}$$

where $VSL_{c,n}$ is the estimated VSL for country c in year n, VSL_{OECD} is the average base VSL in the sample of OECD countries with VSL studies ($3.83 million), $Y_{c,n}$ is GDP per capita in country c in year n, Y_{OECD} is the average GDP per capita for the sample of OECD countries ($37,000), and ϵ is the income elasticity of 1.2 for LMICs and 0.8 for high-income countries. All values are in PPP prices. For VSL in US dollars, $VSL_{c,n}$ is therefore multiplied by the ratio of PPP conversion factor to nominal exchange rates, available in the World Development Indicators from the World Bank.

REFERENCES

Lindhjem, H., S. Narvud, N. A. Braathen, and V. Biausque. 2011. "Valuing Mortality Risk Reductions from Environmental, Transport, and Health Policies: A Global Meta-Analysis of Stated Preference Studies." *Risk Analysis* 31 (9): 1381–407.

Narain, U., and C. Sall. 2016. *Methodology for Valuing the Health Impacts of Air Pollution: Discussion of Challenges and Proposed Solutions*. A World Bank Study. Washington, DC: World Bank.

Navrud, S., and H. Lindhjem. 2010. *Meta-Analysis of Stated Preference VSL Studies: Further Model Sensitivity and Benefit Transfer Issues*. ENV/EPOC/WPNEP(2010)10/FINAL. Environment Directorate. Paris: OECD.

OECD (Organisation for Economic Co-operation and Development). 2012. *Mortality Risk Valuation in Environment, Health, and Transport Policies*. Paris: OECD.

World Bank. 2020. "The Global Health Cost of Ambient PM$_{2.5}$ Air Pollution." World Bank, Washington, DC.

World Bank and IHME (Institute for Health Metrics and Evaluation). 2016. *The Cost of Air Pollution: Strengthening the Economic Case for Action*. Washington, DC: World Bank.

Valuation of Morbidity

Two valuation techniques are commonly used to estimate the cost of morbidity or illness. The cost-of-illness (COI) approach includes cost of medical treatment and value of income and time lost to illness. The second approach equates cost of illness to individuals' WTP for avoiding an episode of illness. Therefore, the latter includes the welfare cost of pain and suffering from illness.

Studies in many countries have found that individuals' WTP to avoid an episode of an acute illness is generally much higher than the cost of treatment and value of income and time losses (Alberini and Krupnick 2000; Cropper and Oates 1992; Dickie and Gerking 2002; Wilson 2003).

The OECD, in its report on the global economic consequences of outdoor air pollution, includes the cost of both mortality and morbidity (OECD 2016). Mortality is valued using VSL, and the cost of morbidity is estimated both in terms of

- Market impacts or COI (reduced labor productivity and increased health expenditures associated with bronchitis, asthma, hospital admissions, and restricted activity days from illness); and
- Nonmarket impacts (welfare cost of pain and suffering from illness).

Globally, the OECD estimated the cost of market impacts or COI to be about 0.2 percent of GDP or equivalent to 4 percent of the cost of mortality. Expressed in terms of welfare, using the equivalent variation of income, the cost was 0.4 percent of GDP or 8 percent of the cost of mortality. The nonmarket impacts or welfare cost was equivalent to 0.5 percent of GDP or 9 percent of mortality cost. Thus, the total cost of morbidity was estimated at 0.7 to 0.9 percent of GDP or 13 to 17 percent of the cost of mortality according to the OCED report.

The morbidity cost relative to mortality cost may now be expected to be higher than estimated in OECD (2016), since GBD 2019 includes type 2 diabetes as an effect of $PM_{2.5}$ exposure. YLDs from type 2 diabetes constitute as much as 31 percent of YLDs from $PM_{2.5}$ exposure in 2019.

Estimating the cost of morbidity requires much more data—and less accessible data, including baseline health data—than estimating the cost of mortality.

Therefore, a simplified approach is applied in this report using the following steps:

- YLDs from PM$_{2.5}$ exposure from the GBD 2019 study are converted to days of illness by applying the disability weights in the GBD studies.
- The cost of a day of illness is then approximated as a fraction of the average daily wage rates to reflect income losses from illness, health expenditures, time losses, and the welfare costs of pain and suffering.
- The cost of a day of illness is also applied to individuals without income because illness prevents most of these individuals from undertaking household work and other activities with a social value, as well as involves all the non-income impacts of illness.

The cost of morbidity is thus estimated as follows. First, annual disease days (M) in country, k, are calculated as:

$$M_k = \sum_{i=1}^{n} M_{ki} = \sum_{i=1}^{n} (YLD_{ki} * 365 / d_{ki}) \tag{D.1}$$

where YLD_{ki} is years lost to disease, i, from exposure to PM$_{2.5}$, and d_{ki} is the disability weight for disease, i, in country, k. The disability weight is from the GBD 2019 for each of seven diseases associated with PM$_{2.5}$ exposure.

The disability weight is a measure used in GBD to calculate YLDs from days of illness, disease, or injury. The weighted average global disability weights for the seven diseases associated with exposure to PM$_{2.5}$ range from 0.027 for ischemic heart disease (IHD) to 0.175 for stroke (table D.1).

The cost of a day lived with disease, i, or a disease day, in country, k, is thus:

$$c_{ki} = w_k \, d_{ki} / D \tag{D.2}$$

where w_k and d_{ki} are average daily wage rate and disability weight for disease, i, in country, k, and D is a disability weight that corresponds to a severity of disease for which the cost of a disease day is assumed equal to the average wage rate. D is here set at 0.4. This is a disability weight (DW) associated with severely restricted work and leisure activity from disease and substantial medical cost, for example, severe COPD (DW = 0.41), distance-vision blindness (DW = 0.19) and stage 5 chronic kidney disease (DW = 0.57) due to diabetes, and stroke with severity level 3 (DW = 0.32) and 4 (DW = 0.55).

TABLE D.1 **Disability weights associated with PM$_{2.5}$ Air pollution**

DISEASE	AVERAGE DISABILITY WEIGHT
Chronic obstructive pulmonary disease (COPD)	0.093
Type 2 diabetes	0.080
Ischemic heart disease (IHD)	0.027
Lower respiratory infections (LRI)	0.060
Stroke	0.175
Lung cancer (LC)	0.169
Cataracts	0.069

Source: Based on data from IHME, GBD 2019 study.

Cost of morbidity (C) in country, k, is calculated as follows:

$$C_k = \sum_{i=1}^{n} (c_{ki}\, M_{ki})\qquad\text{(D.3)}$$

Average daily wage rate is estimated as follows:

$$w_k = GDP_k\,/\,L_k\,/\,250 * s_k\qquad\text{(D.4)}$$

where *GDP* is the country's total GDP, *L* is total labor force, *s* is labor compensation share of GDP, and annual working days is averaging 250. *GDP* and *L* are from the World Development Indicators (World Bank) and *s* is from Penn World Table, version 9.

REFERENCES

Alberini, A., and A. Krupnick. 2000. "Cost-of-Illness and Willingness-to-Pay Estimates of the Benefits of Improved Air Quality: Evidence from Taiwan." *Land Economics* 76: 37–53.

Cropper, M., and W. Oates. 1992. "Environmental Economics: A Survey." *Journal of Economic Literature* 30: 675–740.

Dickie, M., and S. Gerking. 2002. "Willingness to Pay for Reduced Morbidity. Paper presented at the Workshop "Economic Valuation of Health for Environmental Policy: Assessing Alternative Approaches," Orlando, Florida, March 18–19.

GBD 2019 Risk Factors Collaborators. 2020. "Global Burden of 87 Risk Factors in 204 Countries and Territories, 1990–2019: A Systematic Analysis for the Global Burden of Disease Study 2019." *Lancet* 396: 1223–49.

OECD (Organisation for Economic Co-operation and Development). 2016. *The Economic Consequences of Outdoor Air Pollution.* Paris: OECD.

Penn World Table. n.d. Version 9. Groningen Growth and Development Centre. University of Groningen. https://www.rug.nl/ggdc/productivity/pwt/pwt-releases/pwt9.1

Wilson, C. 2003. "Empirical Evidence Showing the Relationships Between Three Approaches for Pollution Control." *Environmental and Resource Economics* 24: 97–101.

World Bank. n.d. World Development Indicators. https://datatopics.worldbank.org /world-development-indicators/.

Bibliography

Alberini, A., and A. Krupnick. 2000. "Cost-of-Illness and Willingness-to-Pay Estimates of the Benefits of Improved Air Quality: Evidence from Taiwan." *Land Economics* 76: 37–53.

Andrée, P. J. 2020. "Incidence of COVID-19 and Connections with Air Pollution Exposure: Evidence from the Netherlands." Policy Research Working Paper 9221, World Bank, Washington DC.

Bowe, B., Y. Xie, T. Li, Y. Yan, H. Xian, and Z. Al-Aly. 2018. "The 2016 Global and National Burden of Diabetes Mellitus Attributable to $PM_{2.5}$ Air Pollution." *Lancet Planetary Health* 2 (7): e301–e312.

Brauer, M., M. Amann, R. T. Burnett, A. Cohen, F. Dentener, M. Ezzati, S. B. Henderson, M. Krzyzanowski, R. V. Martin, R. Van Dingenen, A. van Donkelaar, and G. D. Thurston. 2012. "Exposure Assessment for Estimation of the Global Burden of Disease Attributable to Outdoor Air Pollution." *Environ Sci Technol* 46 (2): 652–60.

Brauer, M., G. Freedman, J. Frostad, A. van Donkelaar, R. V. Martin, F. Dentener, R. van Dingenen, K. Estep, H. Amini, J. S. Apte, K. Balakrishnan, L. Barregard, D. Broday, V. Feigin, S. Ghosh, P. K. Hopke, L. D. Knibbs, Y. Kokubo, Y. Liu, S. Ma, L. Morawska, J. L. Sangrador, G. Shaddick, H. R. Anderson, T. Vos, M. H. Forouzanfar, R. T. Burnett, and A. Cohen. 2016. "Ambient Air Pollution Exposure Estimation for the Global Burden of Disease 2013." *Environ Sci Technol* 50 (1): 79–88.

Burnett, Richard T., C. Arden Pope III, Majid Ezzati, Casey Olives, Stephen S. Lim, Sumi Mehta, Hwashin H. Shin, Gitanjali Singh, Bryan Hubbell, Michael Brauer, H. Ross Anderson, Kirk R. Smith, John R. Balmes, Nigel G. Bruce, Haidong Kan, Francine Laden, Annette Prüss-Ustün, Michelle C. Turner, Susan M. Gapstur, W. Ryan Diver, and Aaron Cohen. 2014. "An Integrated Risk Function for Estimating the Global Burden of Disease Attributable to Ambient Fine Particulate Matter Exposure." *Environmental Health Perspectives*: 122 (4): 397–403.

Carey, I. M., H. R. Anderson, R. W. Atkinson, S. D. Beevers, D. G. Cook, D. P. Strachan, D. Dajnak, J. Gulliver, and F. J. Kelly. 2018. "Are Noise and Air Pollution Related to the Incidence of Dementia? A Cohort Study in London, England." *BMJ Open* 8: e022404.

Chen, J., and G. Hoek, 2020, "Long-Term Exposure to PM and All-Cause and Cause-Specific Mortality: A Systematic Review and Meta-analysis." *Environment International*, Volume 143, https://doi.org/10.1016/j.envint.2020.105974.

Cropper, M., and W. Oates. 1992. "Environmental Economics: A Survey." *Journal of Economic Literature* 30: 675–740.

Dickie, M., and S. Gerking. 2002. "Willingness to Pay for Reduced Morbidity. Paper presented at the Workshop "Economic Valuation of Health for Environmental Policy: Assessing Alternative Approaches," Orlando, Florida, March 18–19.

Ezzati, M., A. D. Lopez, A. A. Rodgers, and C. J. Murray. 2004. *Comparative Quantification of Health Risks: Global and Regional Burden of Disease Attributable to Selected Major Risk Factors.* Geneva: WHO.

Ezziane, Z. 2013. "The Impact of Air Pollution on Low Birth Weight and Infant Mortality." *Review of Environmental Health* 28 (2–3): 107–15.

GBD 2013 Risk Factors Collaborators. 2015. "Global, Regional, and National Comparative Risk Assessment of 79 Behavioural, Environmental and Occupational, and Metabolic Risks or Clusters of Risks in 188 Countries, 1990–2013: A Systematic Analysis for the Global Burden of Disease Study 2013." *Lancet* 386: 2287–323.

GBD 2015 Risk Factors Collaborators. 2016. "Global, Regional, and National Comparative Risk Assessment of 79 Behavioural, Environmental and Occupational, and Metabolic Risks or Clusters of Risks, 1990–2015: A Systematic Analysis for the Global Burden of Disease Study 2015." *Lancet* 388: 1659–724.

GBD 2016 Risk Factors Collaborators. 2017. "Global, Regional, and National Comparative Risk Assessment of 84 Behavioural, Environmental and Occupational, and Metabolic Risks or Clusters of Risks, 1990–2016: A Systematic Analysis for the Global Burden of Disease Study 2016." *Lancet* 390: 1345–422.

GBD 2017 Risk Factors Collaborators. 2018. "Global, Regional, and National Comparative Risk Assessment of 84 Behavioural, Environmental and Occupational, and Metabolic Risks or Clusters of Risks for 195 Countries and Territories, 1990–2017: A Systematic Analysis for the Global Burden of Disease Study 2017." *Lancet* 392: 1923–94.

GBD 2019 Risk Factors Collaborators. 2020. "Global Burden of 87 Risk Factors in 204 Countries and Territories, 1990–2019: A Systematic Analysis for the Global Burden of Disease Study 2019." *Lancet* 396: 1223–49.

GBD 2019 Viewpoint Collaborators. 2020. "Five Insights from the Global Burden of Disease Study 2019." *Lancet.* 396: 1135–59.

Heft-Neal, S., J. Burney, E. Bendavid, and M. Burk. 2018. "Robust Relationship Between Air Quality and Infant Mortality in Africa." *Nature* 559 (7713): 254–58.

HEI (Health Effects Institute). 2020. *State of Global Air 2020.* Boston: HEI. www.stateofglobalair.org.

Landrigan, P. J., R. Fuller, N. J. R. Acosta, O. Adeyi, R. Arnold, N. N. Basu, A. B. Baldé, R. Bertollini, S. Bose-O'Reilly, J. I. Boufford, P. N. Breysse, T. Chiles, C. Mahidol, A. M. Coll-Seck, M. L. Cropper, J. Fobil, V. Fuster, M. Greenstone, A. Haines, D. Hanrahan, D. Hunter, M. Khare, A. Krupnick, B. Lanphear, B. Lohani, K. Martin, K. V. Mathiasen, M. A. McTeer, C. J. L. Murray, J. D. Ndahimananjara, F. Perera, J. Potočnik, A. S. Preker, J. Ramesh, J. Rockström, C. Salinas, L. D. Samson, K. Sandilya, P. D. Sly, K. R. Smith, A. Steiner, R. B. Stewart, W. A. Suk, O. C .P. van Schayck, G. N. Yadama, K. Yumkella, and M. Zhong. 2018. "The Lancet Commission on Pollution and Health." *Lancet* 391 (10119): 462–512.

Larsen, B. 2014. "Benefits and Costs of the Air Pollution Targets for the Post-2015 Development Agenda." Air Pollution Assessment Paper, Post-2015 Consensus Project. Copenhagen: Copenhagen Consensus Center. https://www.copenhagenconsensus.com/sites/default/files/air_pollution_assessment_-_larsen.pdf.

Larsen, B. 2017. *Global Ambient Air Pollution: New Perspectives on Exposure, Health Effects and Costs – Global, Regional and National Estimates for 2015.* A World Bank Study. Washington, DC: World Bank.

Larsen, B. 2018. *The Global Cost of Ambient PM₂.₅ Air Pollution in 2017.* A World Bank Study. Washington, DC: World Bank.

Lim, S. S., T. Vos, A. D. Flaxman, et al. 2012. "A Comparative Risk Assessment of Burden of Disease and Injury Attributable to 67 Risk Factors and Risk Factor Clusters in 21 Regions, 1990–2010: A Systematic Analysis for the Global Burden of Disease Study 2010." *Lancet* 380: 2224–60.

Lindhjem, H., S. Narvud, N. A. Braathen, and V. Biausque. 2011. "Valuing Mortality Risk Reductions from Environmental, Transport, and Health Policies: A Global Meta-Analysis of Stated Preference Studies." *Risk Analysis* 31 (9): 1381–407.

Mehta, S., H. Shin, R. Burnett, T. North, and A. Cohen. 2013. "Ambient Particulate Air Pollution and Acute Lower Respiratory Infections: A Systematic Review and Implications for Estimating the Global Burden of Disease." *Air Qual Atmos Health* 6: 69–83.

Narain, U., and C. Sall. 2016. *Methodology for Valuing the Health Impacts of Air Pollution: Discussion of Challenges and Proposed Solutions.* A World Bank Study. Washington, DC: World Bank.

Navrud, S., and H. Lindhjem. 2010. *Meta-Analysis of Stated Preference VSL Studies: Further Model Sensitivity and Benefit Transfer Issues.* ENV/EPOC/WPNEP(2010)10/FINAL. Environment Directorate. Paris: OECD.

OECD (Organisation for Economic Co-operation and Development). 2012. *Mortality Risk Valuation in Environment, Health, and Transport Policies.* Paris: OECD.

OECD (Organisation for Economic Co-operation and Development). 2016. *The Economic Consequences of Outdoor Air Pollution.* Paris: OECD.

Orellano, P., J. Reynoso, N. Quaranta. 2021. "Short-Term Exposure to Sulphur Dioxide (SO2) and All-Cause and Respiratory Mortality: A Systematic Review and Meta-Analysis." *Environment International*, Volume 150. https://doi.org/10.1016/j.envint.2021.106434.

Orellano, P., J. Reynoso, N. Quaranta, A. Bardach, and A. Ciapponi, 2020. "Short-Term Exposure to Particulate Matter (PM10 and $PM_{2.5}$), Nitrogen Dioxide (NO_2), and Ozone (O_3) and All-Cause and Cause-Specific Mortality: Systematic Review and Meta-Analysis." *Environment International*, Volume 142. https://doi.org/10.1016/j.envint.2020.105876.

Ostro, B., J. V. Spadaro, S. Gumy, P. Mudu, Y. Awe, F. Forastiere, and A. Peters. 2018. "Assessing the Recent Estimates of the Global Burden of Disease for Ambient Air Pollution: Methodological Changes and Implications for Low- and Middle-Income Countries." *Environmental Research* 166: 713–25.

Ostro, B., Y. Awe, and E. Sánchez-Triana. 2021. *Implications of Exposure to Dust on the Burden of Disease from Air Pollution.* A World Bank Study. Washington, DC: World Bank.

Pope, C. A., III, R. T. Burnett, D. Krewski, M. Jerrett, Y. Shi, E. E. Calle, and M. J. Thun. 2009. "Cardiovascular Mortality and Exposure to Airborne Fine Particulate Matter and Cigarette Smoke: Shape of the Exposure-Response Relationship." *Circulation* 120: 941–48.

Pope, C. A., III, R. T. Burnett, M. J. Thun, E. E. Calle, D. Krewski, K. Ito, and G. Thurston. 2002. "Lung Cancer, Cardiopulmonary Mortality, and Long-Term Exposure to Fine Particulate Air Pollution." *Journal of the American Medical Association* 287: 1132–41.

Pope, C. A., III, R. T. Burnett, M. Turner, A. Cohen, D. Krewski, M. Jerrett, S. M. Gapstur, and M. J. Thun. 2011. "Lung Cancer and Cardiovascular Disease Mortality Associated with Ambient Air Pollution and Cigarette Smoke: Shape of the Exposure-Response Relationships." *Environmental Health Perspectives* 119 (11): 1616–21.

Sánchez-Triana, E., S. Enriquez, B. Larsen, P. Webster, and J. Afzal. 2015. *Sustainability and Poverty Alleviation: Confronting Environmental Threats in Sindh, Pakistan.* Directions in Development. Washington, DC: World Bank.

Shaddick, G., M. L. Thomas, A. Green, M. Brauer, A. van Donkelaar, R. Burnett, H. Chang, A. Cohen, R. Van Dingenen, C. Dora, S. Gumy, Y. Liu, R. Martin, L. A. Waller, J. West, J. V. Zidek, and A. Prüss-Ustün. 2018. "Data Integration Model for Air Quality: A Hierarchical Approach to the Global Estimation of Exposures to Ambient Air Pollution." *Journal of the Royal Statistical Society. Series C, Applied Statistics 2018* 67: 231–53.

Shin, H., A. Cohen, C. A. Pope III, M. Ezzati, S. S. Lim, B. Hubbel, and R. T. Burnett. 2013. "Critical Issues in Combining Disparate Sources of Information to Estimate the Global Burden of Disease Attributable to Ambient Fine Particulate Matter Exposure." Working Paper prepared for Harvard Center for Risk Analysis "Methods for Research Synthesis: A Cross-Disciplinary Workshop," October 3.

Shin J., J. Y. Park, and J. Choi. 2018. "Long-Term Exposure to Ambient Air Pollutants and Mental Health Status. A Nationwide Population-Based Cross-Sectional Study." *PLOS One* 13 (4): e0195607.

Shindell, D., J. C. I. Kuylenstierna, E. Vignati, R. van Dingenen, M. Amann, Z. Klimont, S. C. Anenberg, N. Muller, G. Janssens-Maenhout, F. Raes, J. Schwartz, G. Faluvegi, L. Pozzoli, K. Kupiainen, L. Höglund-Isaksson, L. Emberson, D. Streets, V. Ramanathan, K. Hicks, N. T. K. Oanh, G. Milly, M. Williams, V. Demkine, and D. Fowler. 2012. "Simultaneously Mitigating Near-Term Climate Change and Improving Human Health and Food Security." *Science* 335: 183–89.

Shupler, M., W. Godwin, J. Frostad, P. Gustafson, R. E. Arku, and M. Brauer. 2018. "Global Estimation of Exposure to Fine Particulate Matter (PM$_{2.5}$) from Household Air Pollution." *Environment International* 120: 354–63.

Thurston, G., Y. Awe, and E. Sánchez-Triana. 2021. *Are All Air Pollution Particles Equal? How Constituents and Sources of Fine Air Pollution Particles (PM$_{2.5}$) Affect Health.* A World Bank Study. Washington, DC: World Bank.

Van Donkelaar, A., R. Martin, M. Brauer, and B. Boys. 2015. "Use of Satellite Observations for Long-Term Exposure Assessment of Global Concentrations of Fine Particulate Matter." *Environmental Health Perspectives* 123: 135–43.

Van Donkelaar, A., R. V. Martin, M. Brauer, N. C. Hsu, R.A. Kahn, R. C. Levy, A. Lyapustin, A. M. Sayer, and D. M. Winker. 2016. "Global Estimates of Fine Particulate Matter Using a Combined Geophysical-Statistical Method with Information from Satellites, Models, and Monitors." *Environmental Science and Technology* 50: 3762–72.

WHO (World Health Organization). 2009. *Estimated Deaths and DALYs Attributable to Selected Environmental Risk Factors, by WHO Member States, 2004.* http://www.who.int/quantifying_ehimpacts/national/countryprofile/intro/en/index.htm.

WHO (World Health Organization). 2016. *Ambient Air Pollution: A Global Assessment of Exposure and Burden of Disease.* Geneva: WHO.

Wilson, C. 2003. "Empirical Evidence Showing the Relationships Between Three Approaches for Pollution Control." *Environmental and Resource Economics* 24: 97–101.

World Bank. 2020. *The Global Health Cost of Ambient PM$_{2.5}$ Air Pollution.* Washington, DC: World Bank.

World Bank and IHME (Institute for Health Metrics and Evaluation). 2016. *The Cost of Air Pollution: Strengthening the Economic Case for Action.* Washington, DC: World Bank.

Xu, X., S. U. Ha, and R. Basnet. 2016. "A Review of Epidemiological Research on Adverse Neurological Effects of Exposure to Ambient Air Pollution." *Frontiers in Public Health* 4: 157.

Zhang, X., X. Chen, and X. Zhang. 2018. "The Impact of Exposure to Air Pollution on Cognitive Performance." *Proceedings of the National Academy of Sciences* 115 (37): 9193–97.